LORD OF THE RAFTERS

By
Kevin Prochaska

Copyright © 2013, Kevin Prochaska

All rights reserved.
No part of this book may be reproduced, stored in a retrieval system, or transmitted by any means, electronic, mechanical, photocopying, recording, or otherwise, without written permission from the author.

ISBN 978-1-625-17136-8

Of course, who am I to be preaching anything to anyone? Here I am, raised to be God-fearing, but choosing instead to be a thief. I'm hiding in an attic with a rat, wearing a white robe with a half-eaten Baby Ruth in the pocket and talking to a glob of silver. I am the Lord of the Rafters and this is my kingdom.

1

I can feel you behind me, close as a second skin. No warmth of breath betrays you, but I know you are there. Look up then, beyond my yellowed hair. Can you see it?

It dangles way up there above it all, staring down like the sun rising up on Judgment Day. Like somebody just up and nailed it to that lonely sky, except you can't see the nail, or even the string it's hanging from. And see the clouds brushing against it, like a cat against a waiting leg, like it was shaking off the dust, getting ready for the first to be judged. The arms, open, stretch out to offer, as did the man, they tell me, who welcomed even as he was offered. And if you stare up at it long enough, your eyes trick, thinking that it's swaying back and forth with the wind, instead of being just a "t" carved of dull stone. It ain't real, I tell you. Stones don't blow in the wind. And if that's what's true, then all the "t" stands for is something that ain't there and never was. And all who follow the "t" are living that illusion as well.

It is there in the evening, at my time of departure. My eyes gouge into the ground, but always they gaze back skyward. My soul thirsts for the night, and in the half-light, this stone idol comforts me. Why is he what he is, and not what my wants beg him to be? My footsteps pad softly on. He is what he is, they tell me, in order for this whole thing to work. The thought angers me, but nevertheless, a wicked smile creeps onto my face. There is more wisdom than peril in keeping an enemy close.

It hangs in the sky alone, this annoying little letter, not even in its proper form. A hiltless sword, its blade slashing out in opposing directions; it is the conduit through which Heaven and Hell argue their point.

But would not some other letter have served as well?

I *hated* phonics. Let's sound out this letter and then sound out that letter, and do them again and again and again, until your head spins and your stomach gets to churning. And make your mouth very round when you pronounce that "O" letter so you can look like a ridiculous hooty owl as you are doing so, and make sure you say each word re-eal slo-o-ow, so everyone can hear you, crisp and clear as the snapping of a cornflake. Phooey on that. Phooey, phooey, phooey. And double-phooey on getting laughed at by your classmates. What the heck does a second-story man need all that for? Don't do much talking in my line of work.

And don't need nothing dangling in the sky to remind me of times gone by. They're not coming back. Ghosts are better off dead, ain't they? And anyway, since the dude's head was slouching over up there, shouldn't that be an "f" dangling up there if you're truly representing the man and not the wood holding him? Of course "f" begins "failure" and nobody wants to take up *that* cross, I expect. But that's not up to me. The mistake was made a long time ago, and it seems we're all stuck with it.

2

The wind pierces the darkness, kissing my face and cooling my skin as the night absorbs me. My breath leaks through nose and mouth, ghostly white clouds in the February air. The outline of my head creeps down an alley on newly-oiled shoes. A million kinks of thin wire corkscrew around my scalp and a frail beam from some streetlight surrounds straw-colored curls like the halo of a saint. I chuckle. Halo of a saint, right.

My donkey part carries a small canvas satchel, tools muffled in rags within. I continue, faint moonlight glowing from the back of my head, an enormous dirty tennis ball. I know well the course of the black river and wisely steer toward its center. I row on, the river moving me swiftly. My vessel banks sharply to the left and I am there.

It rises as a giant before me and the hairs prickle on my arms. Hospitals do not like me. Doctors turn their backs to me. Nurses vomit at my approach. Thankfully, this place is for the children. They, too, bleed and suffer and need. I don't want to see it—the pain, the crying, the blood. And in this sea of pain, the sacrifice of birth—the cries of the bleeding mother as she coughs forth the child. I won't be a part of it; won't witness the slaughter that it brings. I won't.

My gaze shifts downward, to the prize. It cowers beneath the giant, a mere story in height, an oddity among the majesty surrounding it. Old, crumbling, and encased in steel bars of black, the spirits of whiskey taunt the nostrils and tease the tongue. Anxious metal jingles in my satchel. They should have taken the offer.

Footsteps pad in the darkness. Weak blue and amber lights glow from the glass tavern front—my school colors. A grin crosses my face. *Go Warriors, go Warriors. Fight, fight, fight. Do it up, do it up, do it up right, right, right.* A good omen.

A star in the east shines above me and I pause to admire. Lead on, Brave Star. The star hides, embarrassed. A second star, lower than the horizon, twinkles for a moment and then dims. Stars don't shy their faces from the night sky. And stars don't twinkle in alleyways. I slink away, the devil to pay.

3

The "t" is still hanging there, set against the night by a bright light coming from the spire. An "f" would more signify his life, I still argue, but who am I? Although, come to think of it, some of my favorite words begin with that letter—tacos, television, and tools—a second-story man sure needs tools. And tomatoes, which I'd like to throw at my second-grade phonics teacher, Mrs. Deerdore, mouth former that she was.

It stares down at me and I grow angry, my breath frothy. My finger pecks the night air like the beak of a hungry crow.

"Do not condemn me just 'cause they condemned you!" my muffled voice declares. "It wasn't me!"

The "t" remains silent, but calls to me just the same. In my profession, there is a price for failure. I know that. And I'll take blame for my crimes—but just mine. I'm not taking the rap for a crime that old and that did not involve my people.

Fingers thud against the hollow of my chest and scold the "t."

"If you think you got problems dyin' as you, bro, try livin' as me."

My anger subsides in the cool of the air and I smile at my victory. I have forged this stone sword into a shield. For goodness lurks near crosses, protecting me. Who would find evil beneath a cross? And for seven years, the cross has been loyal to me. I am a man of faith—an abiding faith that if I hide beneath the "t," the High Priests of Black and White will not come for me.

However, betrayed by a star in the east, I still have no loaves or fishes. My eyes climb down from the cross, leaving the nails in place.

4

It's kind of a funny-looking place—the school, that is. Doesn't look like it fits anywhere, kind of like me. Long building, short on character. Just kind of sits out there, like it's waiting for someone to come by and knock it down. Used to be that the outside was concrete blocks stacked row on row, but they covered that up with a thick coat of stucco they sprayed on just like they were just sprucing up the place with paint. Did make it nicer, though; I got to say that much. And look at that roof, would you? Ever see a red roof on a school? Lord, that's a nasty color. Looks like blood flowing over a waterfall, especially with that God-awful pitch they put on it when they built it. Sure wakes those kids up before they come through the door, though, afraid of getting smelly wet blood splashed all over them. Scares them to righteousness when they see all that red. I should know.

I'm not supposed to be looking into the room, but I peek through a window and stand on my toes. Mama is holding her sister's hand as she lies on a bed with her legs scrunched up to her big belly. She is screaming like she's been stabbed with a sword and her face is wracked with pain. There are doctors and nurses crawling all over the place and I see blood dripping on the floor beneath her legs. She screams harder and they're all yelling, "Push, Edna! Push!" She screams so loud I press my hands against my ears, but the screams keep coming. I squeeze my eyes shut as she screams some more, but I open them again. They're pulling something from her belly and my eyes pop out as I see a baby, limp and red with blood. They look at the baby and set it down, and then look at Edna. The room is silent. The baby is still. So is Edna. The blood continues to drip and red roofs do not bother me.

Didn't even start out a school, is what I hear. Started out as a livery stable, and when that burned down, they built a warehouse to store leather shoes and a whole pile of other stuff made from leather. Smells like it, too. Expect they kept some whips there, too, I don't rightly know. Wish they'd quit making whips. Don't do anybody a lick of good. The world could get along just fine without whips, whatever disguise they may come in. Then they built a church next door, and a few years later, the owner of the warehouse sold the place to the church. And that's how that old warehouse, or what was left of it, got to be the Second Street Christian School. Didn't happen all at once, mind you. Took a while, but don't everything but bad?

5

The last time I went to Sunday school was the worst day I ever spent in the holy land. It wasn't what happened at school that was so bad, but what came after that. I came home, all my pretty, colored-up papers in hand, and my mama was on the floor, just slumped against the couch, looking up at me. She raised her hand to me and I knelt down to help her. She kept her hand up, pointing, and when I looked over to see what she was pointing at, I saw a picture of that goat herder she used to pray to, all knotted up with a bunch of pious sheep. She clutched her heart with the other hand. She was breathing hard, and I asked, "Mama, what is it you want me to do?" She pointed to her mouth and said, "Need air, son. Get me some air." So I bent down like I was going to kiss her and started blowing air into her, just like I saw them do on TV. I wasn't scared, because I thought at first she just wanted a kiss—but she wanted more. She wanted me to be God. I blew and I blew, honest I did, and when I saw some color coming to her face, I blew some more. Somewhere during all that blowing, she went limp like a doll, but I never paid no mind. Just kept blowing. Finally, I got tired and straightened up. Looked down at her. Her eyes were open, staring back at me. But I knew she was dead. And then I looked over to the picture of that goat herder, all tied up in piety, and thought that if I had stayed home from Sunday school this one day and not spent all that time getting to know Jesus, I might have saved my poor old mama. My reward for praying up to him was a dead mama. I've never been back to church since then. But I can still see mama talking to the "t," and then telling me the good things to do and the bad things to stay away from. And I do the best I can to obey what she told me to do. Not for his sake, but for hers.

6

I stand before the Sacred Great Glass of the Second Street Christian School. It is the biggest piece of plate glass I have ever seen. Above me a light shines down from the overhang of the blood roof. The glass has captured me.

"Whatchoo lookin' at, fool?" it asks.

I stare back at a half man, half ghoul, with a face carrying anger mixed with a lingering hope of some long-lost pride. The mouth spews smoke like a dragon set to flame. The face before me is black, and whatever its age, it is ten years older than it needs to be. Skin slightly sallow, the cheeks are splashed with darker freckles, large, like a mess of brown scabs. The face is thin and the skin carries scars from lost battles. The skin is darker away from a broad, flat nose. The lips are large, as is the brow. The eyes are blue, clear, and intelligent. The hair, short and kinky, is dirty blond and looks dyed. It is real, but confusing. The body, a paltry fifty-two inches in height, is gaunt and starving. A long, black pullover sweater and beltless black pants cover this almost apparition.

We shift our weight, he to his left leg, me to my right.

Better off all ghost.

The image raises its head toward the sky.

"You couldn't be satisfied, God, just making an off piece of art, could you?" it shouts. "You had to finish it off by making me puny, just like mama was."

The image studies me, top to bottom and then back up.

"What's the matter, Lord? Space getting tight in Heaven?"

I laugh, and from the dragon's mouth erupts a cloud of warning.

A car speeds from the darkness and I launch myself against the Sacred Great Glass, kissing my nightmare.

7

Breaking the Sacred Great Glass is not an option, for doing so would summon the High Priests of Black and White. Each window is tested—each is locked. Footsteps pitter-patter to the far end of the building. The pitter-patter ceases and metal clinks off the back of the half donkey. A sliver of steel bar slides through the satchel opening, offering freedom to the lock. Thrust deftly between the crack in the double doors, my ears are rewarded with a click. My hand grasps the handle and cracks open the door, and a wafer-thin body eases through. Sometimes puny isn't so bad.

I stand beneath the faint red glow of an "EXIT" light, looking down an endless hallway. Through an eternity of boxed tunnel, a second red light marks the far end of the hall. My eyes evolve to those of a hunter peering into a jungle of nothing, and my catlike nose picks up the smell of mildew. Other odors come forward through the dank smell, some real and others familiar ripples of memories long dead. A guilt passes through my soul and I shiver. Should I be doing this? A puff of breeze gently kisses my cheek. Is this not a betrayal? I think of mama and what she did that time, and the guilt passes. I am owed. The loaves and fishes must multiply, and the hell with days gone by.

8

I stand in the doorway of a classroom to my right, peering inside. Overhead lights throw arrow-straight beams of slanted yellow on gleaming rows of new desks. The neat rows of blonde veneer disappear and I sit alone, Mrs. Deerdore fawning over me.

"You're tripping over your tongue, Langston," she says. "It's 'poor' not 'po.'"

I shift on the honey oak seat, the youthful giggles scourging my back until Mrs. Deerdore's cool eyes silence all. My ears ripen as beets, but no one can see the color.

"Try again, Sweetie," she coaxes.

"Po-po-or-poo-rr," I say, my tongue warring with my lips. "Pu-oor-a."

I look up, a baby hooty owl seeking a worm of praise. She shakes her head approvingly.

"Let's try that one more time, Langston."

I will try it as often as you'd like, Mrs. Deerdore, but my tongue is no thicker than it needs to be. My eyes flash to the "t" marching in a line across a field of green paper with all the other baby white alphabet letters. Ask your friend Jesus about that one. My ears burn as those snickers follow me all the way home to mama.

9

My footsteps search cautiously, room by room, rewarded with little more than empty boxes of stale air. Should have figured there was nothing for me here. Was nothing here for me back then.

I enter a larger room and the sweet aroma of latex comes to me. Strange forms rise from the darkness, two dimensional, and over there, three. Hundreds of hearts cut from pink and white paper scattered all over. The art room. I walk through a forest of random and abstract, of tangible thoughts and incomplete dreams. Among the subliminal and the sublime. Behold the minds of children. The latex smell lingers, calming me. My jealous eyes admire their world, one once mine.

I grin stupidly as I stand before them, my reward for being an idiot house darkie instead of an ignorant field blackie.

"Picture Langston, class, not just with your eyes, but with your mind," Mrs. Crumweed instructs. "There is a beauty to his face. Find it. Bring it out, students. Make him a work of art. Make Langston immortal. Put it down on paper."

I sat there for hours, but none of them got it right. Not one. What they saw was a cretin. Swelled lips where there were none. Brillo Pad hair. Freckles the size of Rhode Island. Long, ape fingers. And too much brown. Way too much brown. So much for immortality.

"Very good, class," Mrs. Crumweed complimented. "Very good indeed."

So twenty of my ancestors hung in the hallway for a month, swinging at everyone walking by. Oh sure, some got more points than others, but none of them were me. The only thing they got right was my tongue.

10

There's got to be something worth taking around here. Other rooms to search, but my eyes are pulled to a shape high up on the far wall. It is the "t" and I am compelled to seek out this false work of art. It draws me, calls to me by name. My hand reaches for the cross and I lift it gently from its nail. The moon peeks from beneath a cloud, illuminating the icon in my hand. It is heavy, much heavier than I would have imagined. The body is stiff and shiny, chrome-like in the moonlight. Behind the body hides the tree of death, smooth, with a beautiful, wood-grained finish. It is oak, I think.

The body, tarnished, lies still upon the wood. He sleeps, cradled in my palm, his head tilted to an "f." My thumb runs along his head, feeling the thorns. They are still sharp, even after all these years.

"You couldn't get away from it, either, could you, bro?" I whisper to him.

I run my free hand along the body. It sweats, oily. The cross grows heavier, pushing my hand toward the floor. The wood bounces against my skin as I heft its weight.

"It surely was heavy, bro, wasn't it? Just like that Good Book of yours says."

Way too heavy.

Some fool has scratched the metal. My thumb traces the scratch, pausing to rub it. I should have known better. It is not a scratch. It is the Wound.

And too soft, this flesh of metal. My eyes widen and I gasp.

"I do not know what you've got planned for me in your world, bro, but I know your worth in mine."

Chrome is not soft. And chrome doesn't get dull. But silver does. Solid silver. Multiply then the loaves and fishes.

11

    I ponder my newfound wealth, looking beyond the cross to the art teacher's desk. It sits there alone, this little red ball with a stem.

    I am walking by a fruit stand. Hunger gnaws at my stomach. Rows of forbidden fruit march past me as my tiny, bare feet feel the sidewalk's heat. I look back to find mama. She is looking around. With one quick motion, the Jesus-lover stuffs two of the forbidden fruit into the pocket of her apron.

    I set the cross down and lift the apple from the desk. My eyes dance. The stout stem pokes out from the core. I ease the stem between my thumb and forefinger as the goat herder watches from the cross. I twist gently, and the simple words of a song play for me.

    A-B-C-D-E-F-G-H-

    The goat herder approves, I can tell.

    I-J-K-L-M-

    The stem separates from the apple.

    "M." I should have guessed. Mulatto. That's Spanish for mule. And mules happen when a horse and donkey get to breeding. But mules can't make other mules. They are the dead-end beast. My eyes fall upon his. No fooling, bro? I figure my mama was the horse and my daddy was the donkey, 'cause only a jackass would up and leave a woman to grow a child alone.

    My eyes find his once more.

    "How about you, bro?" I ask. "Your daddy left you out there hanging in the wind, just like mine, didn't he? How do you feel 'bout that?"

    I trace his wound with the stem of the apple. The forbidden fruit floats back to the surface of the desk, for I am no longer hungry.

12

I pick up the cross and study his face.

"Whatchoo lookin' at me like that for, hang man?"

I shake him. In saying nothing, he has said it all.

"So I owe you an explanation, is that what you think? Okay, bro. That's cool."

I prop the cross up against a stack of books and back away, on stage now.

"Okay, since you asked, I'm gonna explain some things to you, goat boy. I'm gonna tell you what's what and how things come down at my end of town."

I wring my hands. They feel greasy. He waits.

"Oh, don't worry, bro, I know your daddy's Top Ten. Learned them long time ago, right here. And mama made sure I knew them—hammered them into my head with the backside of your Good Book. Surprised by that, are you? I've got no strange gods before me, not a single one. And I don't do no swearing. Promised mama that I wouldn't and I don't break promises to mama. Last time I swore was three years ago, when I slammed a pry bar on my pinkie doing a job. But that was it. I haven't sworn since. I don't know what your daddy would say about me using his name in vain, but I know what my mama would say, and that's good enough for me. And I keep that Sabbath day holy. Never do my work then. Good day to watch sports on TV, so why waste it doing break-ins?"

I'm in top form, moving like a boxer as I speak. I continue.

"No killing, either. Never killed anyone—ever. Thought about it, though. But then, who hasn't? Who's never thought that the world would be better off without that one person in it? Makes sense, but still don't do it. And no fooling around with the womenfolk. Another promise I made to mama. I like 'em, I surely do, but most women wouldn't take kindly to my line of work, no how. Now, I've got really good work ethics—it's just my actual work those gals might shy away from. I don't bear false witness. Don't need to lie. 'Cept I don't know how that would work if I ever get hauled in by the High Priests of

Black and White. Ask mama for guidance, I expect—I'd have the time to think, sure would. And I don't covet my neighbor's wife or my neighbor's goods. She's eighty years old for Pete's sake, and wears dentures, and the only thing she's got to pick is that new Lazy Boy she bought at Sears last summer. Try shoving that through a window. Ain't gonna happen. And I don't covet what I steal—who thought up that word anyhow? Sounds like they're talking 'bout a flock of squawking birds or something. I just take it, and I don't know what the take is until I get in there. So how could I covet beforehand? Got that one covered."

He seems satisfied with my words.

"Now, about that stealing commandment, your Jesusship—yea, I take stuff, and it ain't mine, and I ain't about to give it back. I don't hurt nobody in any physical way, and I generally only take stuff from people who got more than I got in the first place. And besides, what happens if I was to sneak back in and try to put that stuff back, and someone up and shoots me? I would have just made that guy sin, and that just wouldn't be right. That poor fool would go to Hell by pure accident."

He seems to understand. I pick up the cross and stare into his closed eyes. He is avoiding me. I bend low, getting beneath his eyes.

"But when you get right down to it, we're all thieves, aren't we, bro? We all take, don't we? It's just the nature of the beast. Mama looked up to you, but mama took so's I could be fed. So how could taking be all that wrong? It's all just stuff of Earth anyhow, ain't it? We're just all using it over and over and over, ain't we?"

The cross rests once more against the books.

"So that's not such a big deal. And I guess if I keep nine of your daddy's Top Ten, I figure I'm batting around .900. You find me any ballplayer swinging the bat that well, bro. I dare you. What's it going to take to get up there in that Almighty Tower with your daddy anyhow? .300? .600? .900? I'm sure Heaven's slopping over with .500 hitters, maybe even some .300 hitters who just picked the right time to retire."

I pause, sticking a thumb to my chest.

"And if you dared let those Klan Kings slip through, you'd best be opening those gates extra wide for yours truly."

He looks as if he might speak, but remains silent. I smile.

"I guess, when things finally shake out, bro, it might all just depend on how you're swinging the bat when the last pitch comes down."

13

Mama Nature just couldn't get the artwork right, no matter what. It seems like she just took all the extra parts left over from her pull-the-half-breed-from-the-hat trick and gave them to me. Frankenstein forehead and Mick Jagger lips. Skin more yellow than brown. And freckles to boot, blots of crusty blood stapled to my cheeks. Nappy, yellow hair that always looks likes it's needing a washing. How many dark skins have got nappy, yellow hair? A sight to behold, I tell you.

I clutch the "t."

"Bet you never had to worry 'bout no one-drop rule, did you, bro?"

My fingers relax from his body.

"But I guess I'm not blaming you, bro. You took the pain."

I look to the ceiling.

"Thank you, God. I owe you one. Thank you, oh Lord, in your almighty generosity, for making me the freak of darkness everyone can get a good chuckle from."

You talk 'bout standing out in a crowd. I'm my own crowd just standing.

Bad enough they got on me on account I'm a half-breed. Yea, they both do—black folk and white. The mule gets the full treatment, not just the half-price special. They both get their licks in. Whoever says only white folks can dole out hate didn't come close to getting it right. Black folks can hate just as good as everyone else. Black folks got nothing on me. They just get to be hated by the whites. I get to be hated by both, and as my reward, I get to hate them both back, but double.

I was always too small to put up much of a fight, and who'd stand up for an overcooked midget anyhow? They teased me about being itsy-bitsy, like the spider—and that's what they hung on me—Itsy Bitsy. Too much in the mouth, though, so that changed, too. Langston Pittman grew up as Bitsy and will be Bitsy to the grave.

I laugh, seeing my tiny coffin waiting in a room filled with larger ones.

And Bitsy in the grave for that matter.

14

Jesus eases into the canvas sack, clinking against my tools. Time to get back to work.

"You don't need to be part of this, bro. Keep *you* batting a thousand, at least."

I turn from the art room, borrowing intangible thoughts, but leaving in my wake the incomplete dreams—I'm not that kind of thief. They bore into my back, asking, "Langston, why didn't you see?"

The darkness greets me once more, and I stand invisible in a hallway so black even the shadows are afraid to come forth. Why are shadows so black anyway? It seems like Heaven itself has stacked the deck against those who wear the dark.

Above me, rows of large vents mixed with acoustic tiles form an uninterrupted pattern in the drop ceiling. On and on they go, down the length of the tunnel, soothing, until my eyes ram hard into some gigantic aberration. It hovers in the right corner at the end of the hall, above the doors where I entered the school. Curious, I moved forward, eyes fixed like bayonets. I am standing below the Big White. It has always been there—I should have remembered. A large, rectangular sheet of plywood painted the color of clouds, as it well should be. For behind this cloud, just a pull of a rope away, ascends the Stairway to Heaven.

I have never been there, but the other kids told me it was up there. And the teachers, smiling, agreed with them. But during all the time I was here, the Stairway never revealed its secrets to me.

Jesus looks up to the Big White, his eyebrows perked in approval.

I raise my hand toward the rope and pull. The Big White creaks begrudgingly toward me, an enormous, hungry mouth opening. My buttocks flex instinctively as the sharp cracking of a whip shatters the air around me. The rope, a leather serpent now, hisses down at me with brass fangs. My terrified hand swats the rope away and I jump backward. The cracking rolls down the tunnel to the Sacred Great Glass, slithering beneath the entrance door. Incomplete dreams? I wore the leather more often than the donkey did.

15

I rub my hand, feeling for the broken fang of the serpent.
Another omen?
Sweat beads drip from my forehead.
My feet track the sound, padding down the tunnel toward the Sacred Great Glass, beyond the school entrance, to the Other Wall. The door saying "Office" has a large, red heart taped to it. I can see it beating in the faint red light of the "EXIT" sign. Beyond the door lies the Not-So-Fun Room. A large, square speaker is mounted to the left of the door, high on the wall, facing the long hallway, and in each classroom hangs its brother. My eyes, fascinated, are nailed to it, its silence beckoning. I wait, anxious to absorb the message, for the Way and the Truth come through here, birthed in the Not-So-Fun Room. Can't say my time spent there was all in vain, though. For imprisoned in that room, in the caged metal of the To-Go Box, wait a bounty of loaves and fishes.
The lock is a child's toy and I open the door. I enter, warning my heart not to jump. No need to now. My eyes penetrate the feeble light and are rewarded with familiarity. Even Mike is still here, a fat, black hot dog standing in the thin air. I am in no hurry. I grin and sit down before Mike. My finger flicks on a large toggle switch and Mike comes to life, like Lazarus back from the dead. My mouth presses close to Mike, and my too-thick tongue partners with my teeth. My lips purge and Mike sucks in the sound. It scurries along the wires like a hurried mouse, to the speaker box high on the Other Wall, and springs into the free air from all its brothers, a prolonged hiss penetrating every molecule in the building. I can hear it, and with the memory of the brass-fanged serpent fresh, the sound frightens me.
"Hsssssss-sssssssssssssssss-sssssssssss.   Hssssss-sssssssssssssss-sssssssssss."
I hesitate, the serpent of the Big White striking, fangs open. I pull back from Mike. But *I* am the Way and the Truth—for right now anyway. I speak.

"Boys and girls, we'd like to take this opportunity tonight to welcome back to the Second Street Christian School your old friend, Langston Pittman, or as you might better know him by, Bitsy. That's right, Bitsy has graciously come back to us tonight, for a limited engagement, or disengagement, if you prefer." I laugh at my veiled joke and I can hear my words reverberating in the hallway tunnel. "We are coming to you live from the Not-So-Fun Room, where we have Principal Babcock all tied up in stitches."

Laughter escapes through each doorway along the hallway, merging into one colossal wave flooding toward me. They are seated in their desks, roaring with laughter. They can see the stodgy principal, gagged to silence, unable to Way and Truth. And I can see their faces, row upon row, and room by room, all eyes tearing with laughter. My victory, partially completed.

Jesus rests in the satchel next to me, and a thought comes to mind. I grin, taking up the cross.

"Boys and girls, do you know what the difference is between Bitsy and Judas?" Mike asks.

I grip the cross, lifting the prize above my head. I shake it.

"Judas got thirty pieces of silver," Mike proclaims. "Bitsy only got one."

I laugh, tickled, as the words roll through the hallway. I drop Jesus back into the sack. A moment for thought. Mike speaks again.

"Where are you, *Chris-ti-ans*?"

Silence. That figures.

"Where are you then, *Chrys-san-them-mums*?" my sarcastic tone evident.

I pick up two pencils, tapping them against Mike. I sing to him, pitching my voice high.

Half-breed, half-breed
Strolling down the track
Trying to get the straight dope
Hidden on my back

My fingers tap the pencils hard against Mike. Tap-tap-tap-tap. Faster. Ta-ta-ta-ta-ta-ta.

Both sides playin' the mule
For just another jack
The low rung of the ladder
A side of beef to stack

He stares up at me from the bag, intimidating. But I know his weakness, of just that once. And he knows I know. The Great Remembrance. Like mama's weakness of just that once. I stare down at the "t," muffling Mike with a hand, and speak to him.

"You old party crasher, you."

Tables knocked violently over, the dull sound of wooden planks clapping against a cut-stone floor. Thousands of coins plummeting and then spinning like tops in a dance of departure. The anger seen only once, but anger just the same. Men in flight, faces in disbelief. "Get out! Get out! Get out!" The one time a whip was justified. And I was there. My heart races, excited by the scene, fingers pressed hard against a heaving chest.

More coins plummet, the sound of metal against stone racing along the wires, faster than the speed of light, flooding the school with a prolonged thunder of silver clinking. I squeeze my hands against my ears until the metallic waterfall runs dry.

16

Mike is resting now, and I kneel in adoration before the To-Go Box. It is heavy and will not move. I play with the dial, pressing an ear against the gray steel door. The tumblers will not drop and I grow impatient. It's a child's toy, like the door. But I am older now, my ears not as sharp. I try again. The tumblers still refuse to drop. I press my face so close to the door, my skin drains away the coldness from the steel. No wonder, my eyes finally tell me. This is not the To-Go Box I knew.

Frustrated, I lean against the wall, panting. I look to Jesus, peeking out from my satchel. I am sweating. He must be, too.

"Warm in there?" I ask.

His body glows in the darkness.

"Should try hell sometime."

For some reason, I find that very funny and I laugh hysterically.

"That's right, bro, I forgot, you already took that trip. Didn't stay too long, though, did you?"

I think I see him blink.

"And if you couldn't hack it, how are the rest of us supposed to?"

I guess that's the whole idea. I pull him out of the bag to the cooler air.

"That better, bro?"

He rests in my hand. The body grows soft and begins to melt, flowing over the wooden cross and onto my hands as a sticky blob of silver jelly, radiant in shine. I shove the blob back, reshaping it, and he climbs back onto the wood.

"You looking for salvation, bro?" I ask. "Here's your prayer then."

My eyes glance toward the dial on the To-Go Box and back to him.

"Get me in there and I will save you. I will leave you here, hanging in your little tree. I promise. You don't want to be melted down now, do you?"

And I didn't want it, either, I guess. But I had to make him understand that. Sting like a bee.

"Come on now, bro, you don't want to lose to the cross twice, do you?"

That one had to hurt.

17

The tumblers still refuse to fall. The eyes of the cross are empty.

"You're only half talking to that daddy of yours up there, bro," I warn. "Best speed it up."

I am familiar with this kind of To-Go Box. I know the combination requires four numbers. And if Jesus doesn't come through for me soon, I'm cooked. But then, so is he. I laugh as the silver shimmers.

The surface of the principal's desk is an orderly clutter of papers, brown files, phone call messages, and other items. It is an altar of no use to me.

I see Jesus now. He is sitting in the shade of a palm tree, his back leaning against its trunk. He bends forward, his finger moving through the dirt. What is he writing? I approach silently, peering over his shoulder. He doesn't know I am there. He completes the motion and lifts his finger. Etched in the yellow dirt is "3."

My eyes stare in question at those of the crucifix. They desert the cross and move to an object on the desk. It couldn't be this easy. Prayers don't get answered.

His finger moves across the dirt once more and I gasp. It is "16."

Carved on an ornate piece of finished wood on the desk twelve inches from my eyes are the words "John 3:16." I study them, knowing I need four numbers to enter the To-Go Box. My mind wanders back through the years, to a blackboard and an abbreviation jotted in chalk. The tips of my fingers grasp the dial on the safe and turn it, stopping on my hunch. I hear the first tumbler drop. I was correct—J is 10. But four numbers are what I need. I glance to "n" and rotate the dial one extra turn to 14. The second tumbler falls. The third and fourth I already have—3 and 16.

I am so clever, I tell myself. The Great Mystery of the Finger in the Dirt has been solved at last. And I was the one who broke the code. Clever, clever Bitsy.

Stupid Bitsy is what *they* all thought. Itsy Bitsy is what *they* called me. Cretin Creature is how *they* drew me. Mumble Mouth. Ton of Tongue. Brillo Boy. Yellow Fellow. Well, I will show them. I will show them all. For I am owed. Pride swells from deep within my soul, releasing the energy of a thousand bombs. I cry out to my hidden shadow and spring to my feet to celebrate the ancient dance of the half horse. Victory is mine sayeth the Lord. I leap high into the air, arms raised in jubilation, in exaltation.

The room I knew then is not that room now. Something has changed, something of dimension. And it is me. For I am taller now. I blast toward the Heavens with the force of a rocket, the antiquated, cast-iron pipe still protruding from the west wall. The pipe attacks my skull with a vengeance and my dark world grows even darker.

18

My footsteps echo in this darkness, unsure of direction. They pause. A glow in the distance guides their path. A cone of light shines upon a stranger standing on a cold cement floor. His back is toward me, bare and dark as ebony. Deep scars run up and down his skin.

An arm reaches to the Heavens like the torch-bearing Statue of Liberty, but clutched in the hand is a wooden shaft, bearing seven thin strips of leather. The hand freezes, wavering ever so slightly, muscles tense. The arm lashes angrily down into the darkness, to a waiting cry of pain, and my body flinches. The crack of leather against raw skin sickens me. My feet move forward. The whip lashes out a second time and a pain-wracked wail again pierces the air. Sweat rolls down the black skin of his back as his whole being arches downward. I circle the cone of light, keeping in the darkness. My eyes study him from the side.

His face turns to me and I am appalled. It is my donkey half, his coal-black face bare of blemish or freckle. The hair is kinky, its oily, black curls shining. The nose is large, the brow pronounced. Thick lips curl wickedly at me and dark eyes burn with a fire stoked by hate. It is my face.

He ignores me, turning away to the other darkness. The whip comes once more. The cone of light shifts and I look down. A man cowers on the floor, shirt stripped, legs curled in the fetal position. Blood flows from long, red cuts on his back. His hair is straight and straw yellow, his skin a sickly white. The half donkey raises the whip and the cowering man stretches out a hand to ward off the blow. His face, covered with blotchy, brown freckles, turns toward me, eyes pleading. The face is that of my half horse.

The whip descends, and from a pained mouth comes the harsh, traitorous crowing of a rooster. Blood squirts from his back, ample drops splashing to a silver body sleeping nearby.

19

An irritating sound awakens me, the sound of a bumper grinding over the cement curb of a parking space. My head pounds and my mind is muddled. Confused eyes search the immediate area, reminding my brain that I am in the Not-So-Fun Room. The door to the To-Go Box is still closed. I lie on the floor, arms outstretched in crucifixion. Jesus rests on the floor to my right, mocking me. Viewed from Heaven, we must be quite a sight.

A car door opens and slams shut a few seconds later.

I shake my head and rise from the floor, dizzy, my eyes wary of the cast-iron pipe. The Not-So-Fun Room is quickly arranged as it had been and I exit, taking Jesus and the satchel. The long hallway, clothed in the early morning light, welcomes me. Slow footsteps slap-slap-slap against the sidewalk next to the building, and keys jingle. Someone sings an unfamilar tune.

It's going to be a golden day
Do your duty
Take your pay

The singing stops abruptly. The footsteps backtrack toward the car.

You ain't gonna leave here anyway

Better get going.

My feet race down the hallway toward the double doors from where I entered, Jesus jiggling against the tools in my satchel. As I reach to push open the door, a milk truck blocks my way. The driver, his back to the door, studies an invoice. He turns, his attention drawn by a shout from around the building. I'm still batting .900, Lord. Let that be a good enough reason not to let them catch me. My eyes look up. Directly above me, I see the Big White. I hear voices outside, louder. The milk will come rolling through the doors within seconds. My legs, uncertain, do half jumps. The rope beckons me, but I am horrified by the cracking of a whip. Milk crates scrape against the floor of the truck bed. My hand reaches up, pulls back empty, but reaches once more. The Big White yawns, the hinges creaking open. The Stairway opens before me and I scurry up, consumed by Heaven. The Big White closes behind me.

    I am panting. The Stairway to Heaven, it seems, is not guarded by a whip.

20

Darkness, the fickle pet, waits besides me, loyal to its own. With him is a friend, for it is cold up here. My body shivers, mouth fuming the vapor cloud of a dragon.

The double doors open and I look down through a vent. Two men enter, the first pushing a handcart stacked with milk while the other holds open the door to let him pass. I recognize one of them and my heart leaps for joy.

Old Fezziwig, alive again.

Mr. Devlin, grayer now, and a bit thinner. Mr. Fix It. Been at the school forever. The loyal, underpaid maintenance man, growing old, but still getting the job done just the same. The limp is new. Bet the kids really snicker behind his back now.

It is not a crime, growing old. Just a pity.

They walk down the hallway and out of sight. A door opens and closes, the sound echoing down the hallway. They are taking the milk to the lunchroom.

I sit in the warmth of my lunch seat, food spread out before me. I open my tiny paw, two shiny pennies nesting on my palm.

"That's enough for a box of white milk, Langston," the lunch lady says.

"But I want chocolate milk," I protest.

"Your mother says you are to drink white milk, young man."

"Suppose she thinks that if I drink chocolate milk my skin's gonna go dark."

My classmates laugh at my joke.

"That's not how it is at all, Langston. You haven't enough for chocolate."

Ain't that the truth.

My pet changes colors with the rising of the sun. Shafts of early morning light filter into the attic from long, slender openings between fascia boards and from the vents in the floor. It is still cold, but warming a bit. I look up.

The backbone of the roof is made up of enormous wooden rafters running at regularly spaced intervals along the length of the school. The rafters hold up the roof as they were meant to do, concentrating their strength as the weight of the roof pushes down on them. Like Atlas holding up the world, they become more stubborn under stress. Each rafter is gigantic, fully eight inches on each side and must weigh a hundred pounds. Opposing rafters rise from the outside walls and are joined at the center with thick steel bolts. A cross joint connects the bolted rafters, providing additional strength, and each set of joined rafters forms an oversized "A." My short frame can stand and walk upright, my head passing easily beneath the cross joints. There are dozens of rafters up here, the wood as dark as me. But I wonder if as stubborn.

21

It grows lighter in the rafters. I rest, shaking the dizziness of the cast-iron collision from my head. My fingers probe the top of my skull, exploring the boundaries of my recently-acquired knot. I have earned a trickle of crusting blood for my efforts. Below me, other doors open and more noise filters up. The teachers are arriving. Voices greet one another, exchanging pleasantries. Individual classrooms light up, one by one, the attic glowing with the rays from below. My nose catches the aromatic smell of freshly brewed coffee and I would sell the remainder of my soul for just one sip. I understand how grateful those guests at Canaan must have been when help arrived to fill their empty wine cups. It has been twelve hours since I last drank and I am thirsty. A hunger claws at my stomach. Perhaps I should have eaten the forbidden fruit in the Garden of Incomplete Dreams.

The voices move along the hallway in groups of two's and three's. They pass by the Sacred Great Glass and form two opposing lines along a strip of pavement. I watch through an open slat in a fascia board. As the teachers chat, they laugh, sipping coffee. They are like children and I envy them. But they are royalty first.

The donkey and the horse kneel before the great King Solomon, the newborn mule lying on the stone floor between them. They look up to the throne, each unwilling to acknowledge the presence of the other. The wise ruler stands, each head nodding in approval as he draws the sword.

A car passes between the lines of teachers, and coming to an orange cone, stops. The driver exchanges greetings with some of the teachers, laughing at something said. One of the teachers opens the car door and a little girl jumps out. She wears a plaid skirt and a white blouse bearing some symbol on the pocket. But I already know what it is. It is the "t" surrounded by a circle. The girl pulls a large backpack from the seat, fully half the size of her own body. It drops to the road with a thud and she struggles to stand it upright. Pulling a handle up, she tilts it backward and rolls it over the curb. She approaches the

Sacred Great Glass and makes a face. A hand motions her to the entrance door.

"Good morning, Miss Harkins," the teacher greets. "First one, as usual."

The young girl makes another face in the glass.

"Come, Trudy," the teacher says, "to the lunchroom."

The young girl passes through the door and is lost inside. A second car stops, emptying three children, and taking longer than the first car. A third car stops behind it, and a fourth behind it. Doors push open and teachers rush to help the children unload. Each car, emptied of its contents, speeds away as the children are ushered inside to the lunchroom, girls wearing white blouses and plaid skirts, boys wearing white shirts with tan trousers. All have the same symbol on the pocket as they chatter away like squirrels.

The car pool continues for half an hour, gradually slowing to lone vehicles making their appearance. These drivers seem rushed, some disheveled. Like a doubting Thomas, they appear to be the last ones to get the word. Children admonished as they depart, heads shaking in wonder, parental eyes rolling. A small girl falls as she jumps from the car, her palms planting flat against the sidewalk. Her backpack slides off the car seat, spilling papers, books, and pencils onto the road. She cries, her knees scratched on the sidewalk. Three teachers surround her, picking up her things and attending to her. The mother looks back, worried.

"It's just a tiny scratch, Mrs. Lawler," a teacher says. "We'll take care of it."

The teacher looks down at the little girl.

"Won't we, Margie?"

The girl nods, holding her knee.

"Are you sure?" asks the mother.

"We'll have the school nurse look at it, right away."

The teacher smiles.

"It's not like it's never happened before."

The mother hesitates, but drives away. The girl is escorted inside, her sniffles fading.

22

The cars stop coming and the teachers reenter the building. I rise and walk along a line of boards laid out like a catwalk below the apex of the rafters. My ears follow the thunder of three hundred voices bouncing from the walls of the lunchroom. My footsteps walk through shadows, the rafters surrounding me as if closing in on their prey. I feel as if I am walking inside the skeleton of some large beast. I chuckle at my thought. Bet Jonah never got a catwalk like I got.

My tongue tastes the grit of sandpaper. I have awakened the dust. I remember the choking desert dust our feet stirred as the long line fled east and the wafers of dried snow that trickled down to feed us during our long, aimless journey. We were the children then.

Stacks of boxes and clumps of unrecognizable items are stored between some of the rafters. Long, square tunnels snake along the floor of the attic, a metal train going nowhere. They are heat ducts.

The voices begin to grow softer, gradually fading to silence.

I backtrack, halting above the row of ceiling vents running above the main hallway. I see them, lines of children funneling neatly into the hall, each blindly following a teacher, a mother hen leading her chicks.

The line of chicks I see below is mostly white, but some Oriental, with a sprinkle of black here and there. I was the whole sprinkle back then. A doorway swallows up each line, and suddenly, the hallway is empty. Noises. Book bags crashing to the floor. Chairs banging against desks. Teasing, laughing, shouts, questions. And above all the noise, the authoritative clucking of the mother hen. A ding-ding-ding sound quells the mayhem, aided by a finger against a teacher's lips.

I remember now. Time for the Way and the Truth.

"Good morning, students and teachers," it begins. "This is Principal Tuttle. We'd like to begin our school day with a prayer. Your teachers have written it on the chalkboard in each classroom. Please pray it out loud and in your heart."

Always a prayer. I remember that part. A younger voice begins, with other voices joining in.

"Oh, Heavenly Father, grant us your protection as we strive to do your will. Favor us when we please you, and pardon us during those times when we fail. Grant us your salvation in the name of your son, Jesus Christ."

My lips move with memory, mouthing the words I had repeated hundreds of times a long time ago, my muttering lost among the voices of the children.

Kind of spooky, praying to something you can't see. Sort of like talking to the wind. And the wind ain't got no ears, that I do know. I mean, if you saw somebody all alone in the middle of a great, big field, and they were talking to the wind, wouldn't you think they'd be better off shipped to the funny farm? My feelings exactly.

"And before we recite the Pledge, here are today's announcements."

I look at his crown of silver head peering up from the opening in my satchel.

"You got yourself quite a fan club down there, don't you, bro?"

23

There is but one voice speaking in each room now. The school day has started and each teacher begins the first class. I ease along the catwalk, peering through the vents into each room, taking in all the activities below me. I watch as one teacher explains a math concept to her students with such simplicity you'd think she was the child telling it to her daddy. Slowly and deliberately, she repeats the mathematical law several times. All eyes are upon her. A pencil performs a ballet across one student's paper, leaving in its wake an ebony trail. When the teacher turns her back to write on the board, two students in the back row engage in a duel with pencils while two others snicker at their antics. The teacher continues to write, calling out their names in admonishment without even looking around. Faces reddening, they put up their swords.

She continues to explain the math. One God, two stone tablets, three Wise Men, four calling birds—ya-dee-da-dee-da. It's all just math, if you want to know the truth about it. Religion is a number's game, and gamblers and tax collectors are right in there with 'em, drinking from the same trough.

My head jerks up suddenly. I hear faint music. But perhaps I really don't hear it yet—perhaps my senses just feel it vibrating through the bones of the rafters. It comes not from tin or wind or brass or from the pounding of a drum. It is the warmest melody of my youth. The instrument plays, but just one note is sounded. Not of the instrument, but of the union of rubber against wood, carrying with it a fragrant smell of profuse sweating. It is the sound of a basketball bouncing on hardwood.

I tried other sports, honest I did. As a football player, I was splayed out like a fish on a filleting table. Tried baseball. Never liked the game. Too much standing around. Soccer was okay, but just okay. But basketball—now that's a game.

Movin' and a'groovin'. Shakin' and a'bakin'. Givin' and a'takin'. Take to task, wear the mask, and don't ask. Layup, double jump, pump n' fake. In your face, ace. Over the head, collect the dead. Off the board, no reward. Off the rim, don't feed to him. In da' net, you bet. Sweet.

I rise from the floor and follow the sound through the tunnel of rafters, the satchel dangling from one hand. I stop briefly to remove the tools from the bag, leaving Jesus alone at my side. The boards below my feet vibrate as a hollow "boomp" sound shakes the attic. The furnace has kicked on, and the heated air, pushed by a huge fan, expands the metal walls of the heat ducts outward. The heat radiates from the metal, warming me when I touch it, and my skin pricks to remind me of the cold. I move forward, the rush of heat pouring through the ducts into the classroom shielding any telltale sound I might make. My path of boards leads me to a wall at the end of the school. I turn right and find a second row of rafters running perpendicular to the first. I follow them and stop at a small window overlooking the gym. Below me is the basketball court on which I first heard the music of the wood. My heart skips in joy. One thing about gyms—they never change through the years. They're like an old friend caught in a time warp, and when you see 'em, they're the exact same as when you saw 'em last.

At one end of the court, a group of girls play, bouncing the ball in clusters of two's and three's. They mean well, but are more intent on talking and giggling among themselves than playing the game of basketball. They keep one eye open for the gym teacher, and when they think he is about to look their way, they begin moving about, passing the ball around like clumsy clowns. Things are very different at the opposite end of the court. Two teams of boys battle on the hardwood. Each team is aggressive, fighting for the ball as the gym teacher shouts out instructions. It is turmoil at its finest, and I love it. The players take many shots, missing most. They scream loudly, raising hands to call for the ball, and run around the court in a mass of tangled arms and legs. I am as excited as they are.

"Go! Go!" I shout, my legs springing. "High to low. Now, jump! Jump! Rebound! Rebound! Rebound!"

Jarred to reality, a hand swings up to muffle my mouth. A boy looks up to my window and I pull back. He squints his eyes and points, but no one pays attention to him.

I am on the court now, all four feet two of me. Moving with the speed of the wind, dirty Keds work to keep up with my feet. Monkey Man leaps into the air, the crowd roaring.

"Go, Monkey Man!" my classmates squeal. "Go!"

I race to the net, my shoes exploding from the hardwood. My calves tighten. I fake jump and the forward commits. Too late, he is in the air to block a shot not taken. Coming down, he sees me spring, his face molded into the expression of, "I've been had." At the top of my jump, my hands push away from my body, releasing the ball. It rises high over the hoop to splash against the backboard. It falls, dropping through the net without touching metal.

"Go, Monkey Man!" they shout. "You go!"

"It's Langston," a voice corrects. "Don't call him that."

"But he jumps as high as any monkey ever could," a young voice defends. "Didn't you see him leap up like that?"

"Nevertheless," the voice replied, "we don't call people names like that."

"But we call him Bitsy all the time," the young voice defends. "Really."

"Well, call him Bitsy then, if you must."

24

Does God wear Keds? Is Heaven of hardwood and three-point lines? One can only hope.

I love the smell of a gym and the music of the ball against the hardwood. Loved it so much I went there after school, regular as a clock. Played against One-on-One Willie all the time. Nice thing about a pull out pal is that he dresses out different every day. He stood before me on Monday as a tall, white Boston Celtic. Tuesday, he was an Afro-haired giant wearing a Lakers jersey. Wednesday, he was a Hoosier junior All American. And day after day, he came on the hardwood to hunt me.

"I'm fixin' on takin' you downtown today, Little Bitsy," he'd sneer.

"Then you gonna need a bigger bus than the one you brung," I'd trash back.

He'd spin the ball on his finger, staring me down.

"I see why they call you Bitsy."

"Ain't nothin' to a name but letters," I'd tell him.

"Let's party then."

"Bring it," I'd reply.

And we would. Didn't matter. Red-haired giants, freckle-faced freaks, seven-foot two dolly bops–didn't make a flip to me. They kept coming, all shades and sizes, and I kept beating 'em. They was all One-on-One Willie, playing the mule. They found him stubborn, like mules are supposed to be, and he drove them from the court mercilessly because stubborn was what he did best.

One-on-One Willie kept me company every afternoon as I waited for the donkey to come pick me up. Waiting was good for me. And I got better and better at the music of the hardwood.

I decided that, one afternoon, I would show the donkey my dance. I would play One-on-One Willie while he watched. He would see me jump and hear the crowd shout out my name. And be proud of me.

The best game never played. He caught the redeye all right, 'cept his trip had nothing to do with no airplane.

25

An empty gym is a lonely place, a hollow grave that spits back the corpse. I turn from the window, my body shivering as I make my way back to the Stairway to Heaven. My eyes fall upon something in the corner, and I make my way toward it.

The main task of an attic is not to hold up a roof, as one might assume—it's put way up above everything as a place to store things. Yep, it's a pretty expensive closet. A stack of boxes sits on a makeshift floor of loose boards, flecks of dust covering the corrugated, brown cardboard. Someone has written on the outside of the boxes. I lean closer, peering to read what it says. The letters spell out the words "Christmas Costumes." The tape on top of one of the boxes has peeled back. I place my sack of Jesus on the floor and pull open the lid. The box is filled with clothing, and seeing it reminds me of the cold air surrounding me. I rummage through the box, my eyes catching a glisten of gold. I pull out a simple white garment. It looks like a long, white bathrobe on which some mother has rough-stitched two rows of thin, gold bands around the wrist-length cuffs. I shiver in the coolness of the attic. I strip a narrow cloth belt from the garment and put the robe on. Its warmth is immediate.

Something else sits next to the boxes, partially hidden. My ears detect a sound and shadows appear to move. I ease my body around the stack, my eyes surprised. Spread out on the floor before me, as if set up as a shrine, is the manger scene. They are all there, every one of them. Arranged with set-piece precision, they remind me of little soldiers waiting for the battle to begin. And perhaps they are. The Christ child sleeps in the manger, little, pink face shining out from a swaddling blanket. Mary and Joseph kneel close by, looking down at him.

"What were you thinking, lady?" I mumble. "You really wanna bring a kid into *this* world?"

My ears hear the cry of a baby and my nose picks up the smell of fresh blood flowing over the roof above my head.

But then I remember—*wanna* wasn't part of the deal.

A group of shepherds stand outside the stable, peering in to see the newborn. Sheep, camels, goats, rabbits, dogs, and numerous species of birds gather around, their attention focused on the child.

I see a donkey and my eyes flash in anger, my little hand flinging it to the floor where it shatters into pieces. I cry on mama's shoulder, and she lets it go unpunished.

Three kings kneel before the manger, holding gifts in their hands. The bottle of frankincense has a deep, ugly gouge in it. An angel floats above the roof of the stable. My mind retreats back through the years, and I stand with my classmates, singing "Angels We Have Heard on High." We are they, set in stone on the floor below me.

My movement has awakened the dust and flecks of it dance in the shafts of light piercing the hollow attic like thin rapiers. I stare at the scene the star of Bethlehem must have gazed down upon. Dressed in my white robe, I am the Belated Shepherd, the one who never got the word. This thought makes me sad.

Why would someone set them up, and way back here? Why not just box it for the year and forget about it, like everyone else does? I do not know the reason, and perhaps whoever did this doesn't, either. But I stand before the stable assemblage, hypnotized by the serenity. A wave of guilt passes through me. I see the innocence of this unblemished baby face, and how it will appear adorned with bloody thorns. But I will not take the blame for a crime that old and that did not involve my people. The sack of Jesus rubs against my thigh and that hypocrisy forces me to turn my face away.

26

He moves slowly, his breath labored. A small, leather tool pouch hangs loosely around his waist. His hand fondles a screwdriver as he limps along the hallway. His feet stop at the doorway to a bathroom and a weak hand pushes open the door, tightening a screw on a hinge. He opens and closes the door several times, hearing the squeak, then pulls a small oilcan from his pouch. A few squirts on the hinge silence the squeak.

He limps back down the hallway, stopping in front of a second doorway. A teacher, her belly bulging out, peeks into the hall. She looks back to her class.

"Keep your eyes on your own work, children."

Her back against one side of the doorframe, she keenly trains one eye on them as her attention turns to the janitor.

"Thanks for taking care of that squeak for us, Grandpa. It was about to drive me to distraction."

"No problem. Anything for my favorite granddaughter. This old building's like a kid itself—always needing attention and always costing money to keep it going."

She smiles.

"You still coming over for dinner on Sunday, right?"

"Wouldn't miss it, Sweetie. You know how I love fried chicken. And that cheesecake you make is the best."

She points to the leather pouch.

"Doesn't that thing weigh you down?"

He shakes his head.

"Never has before. Carried it for all these years."

He pats her stomach and grins.

"You're one to be talking about being weighted down."

A disturbance in the room behind them. She turns to her class.

"If you are finished with your reading, class, take out your workbook and answer the questions on the story." Her head swivels, her eyes shifting to a single student. "And no talking."

"Better get in there," he says. "They'll skin one another if you let them."

"Not *these* little angels," she replied. "You must be talking about some other little angels."

He smiles and turns away, limping along the carpet to disappear around the corner. Across the hall, a second teacher pokes her head out the door.

"How's he doing?" she asks, pointing to her heart.

"He has his days," the granddaughter replies. "Principal Tuttle keeps telling him not to work too hard. And she says we need to keep our tasks for him simple."

Her body jerks and she grabs her midsection.

"He's an active little guy," the other teacher says.

She holds her stomach, smiling.

"Anxious is more like it, I think. He wants out."

"The first one usually seems the most anxious, that's for sure."

A book crashes to the floor.

"And speaking of anxious, I'd better get back to this crowd behind me."

They turn and reenter their respective classrooms, and as they do so, two boys emerge from their hiding place in the bathroom, mischief on their faces. They giggle and scurry up the hallway, to be gobbled up by a doorway.

27

I peer through the vent, observing the pregnant teacher. She is seated on a too-high stool in front of her class. Her body shifts often, like a restless dog moving around in circles, trying to find a perfect place before lowering its body to sleep. She wears a skirt that hikes up her leg more than it should and her stomach sticks out even more that it did when she stood talking with her grandfather. Her obvious misery makes me uncomfortable, and I fidget as I bend over, looking down at her.

Why does it have to be so hard? In my mind, I see the looming shadow of the hospital and my eyes squeeze shut. I see her stretched out on a table, face contorted with pain. She is breathing hard. Her mouth opens and she screams. I feel her pain and fight it. The child is crowning. I won't witness it. I won't. A stable appears, and my eyes open. My hands clutch firmly around my stomach.

I drop my arms and chase the images away.

My stomach growls as the hunger grows. I think of the forbidden fruit and my feet carry me toward it. I stand above the art room, looking down at the desk. The forbidden fruit is still there. A teacher walks among a classroom full of students. Each pupil sits on a stool, an easel of paper propped before them, drawing an arrangement of flowers sitting on a table in front of them. I am grateful my tongue is not on display for their lead-lined rapiers, the only part of me not yet desecrated by pencil point in this room.

"Remember to use the shadows," the teacher says. "Put the shadows where they will do the most good."

I am a master of the shadow, sister. I could teach you a thing or two about how dark things really are.

The furnace kicks on, and the hollow "boomp" reverberates though the attic. The heat flowing from the duct distorts the air, and the forbidden fruit appears to wobble. The teacher moves around the room, critiquing each work, and then settles into her seat. She looks over the class, her eye catching the shine from my apple. She studies her class again and her hand moves toward my prize. She grasps the treasure and my stomach groans. The fruit rises from the table and my wet tongue moistens my lips as I watch. Her hand polishes the apple.

With my luck, her name's probably Eve. I chuckle through my hunger. So I guess this must be what they mean by eavesdropping.

My fingers perch on my lower lip, pushing back hungry drool. Her mouth opens wide. The apple moves forward in slow motion. My eyes close—I do not want to see. Her mouth is mine and I open it, waiting in anticipation to accept the bite. I hear the sharp crunch as her teeth bite into the fruit, played over and over in the milliseconds that follow. I can taste it, feel its juices rolling over my lips. My tongue licks my fingertips as she chews the white ambrosia. She pulls the fruit away and I can see where the bite has ruined this perfect sphere, the exposed white interior teasing my senses.

My eyes fall upon a gigantic, dust-covered mousetrap three feet from the vent. The trap is set, and a piece of dry cracker sticks out from the bait holder. The copper-colored coils patiently await the command to snap shut. I look past the trap. Peering back at me, eyes shining as red as the devil's, squats a gigantic gray rat.

Startled, I push away from the vent, my feet scraping against the loose floorboards. I freeze, staring down the rat, desperately exploring my options should he suddenly attack, while pondering if what I see is real. He flinches and I am sure now. I wonder if the noise I made has been detected below. The rat resumes his role as a statue, staring back at me. He seems unafraid of my size, but I am used to that.

"What's that noise up there?" a boy's voice asks through the vent slits.

"I don't know," a girl answers. "Maybe it's God, letting us know he's watching us."

"Sounds like our friend Rory is back," the teacher says. "That squirrel needs to find another place to hang out."

"Rory is back?" a young female voice asks.

"Maybe we'd better tell Mr. Devlin," a young male voice suggests.

"Maybe we should," the teacher replies. "And, Mr. Matley, you can take him this note I'm writing so he can attend to our Mr. Rory."

It wasn't an ugly nick in the frankincense bottle, I realize. They were teeth marks, and not from a squirrel. The thought of this ugly, gray rodent roaming unchecked through the sanctity of the stable disturbs me.

He must pay for his disrespect.

Two red eyes gaze at me as I ease the stale cracker from the bait holder. The rat watches, betraying no emotion, his nose twitching as my hands crush his lunch into a powder that trickles to the floor as minute grains of dust. He turns and steals away, his endless tail weaving a trail in the dust.

28

I smirk, realizing that if I was that rat looking at me, it must be witnessing an extraordinary sight. Black-skinned dude with yellow hair, dressed in black clothes, and covered with a white bathrobe trimmed in gold, and stealing my lunch no less. No wonder he took off. That hairy mother should be grateful to me, just the same. If he'd bitten off a piece of that cracker, his neck would be snapped in two right about now.

I look around the attic, my eyes wary of his return, but my gaze falls instead upon the closed eyes of the cross at my side.

"Don't feel too bad, bro—I guess my kingdom's ain't of this world, either."

I am on the hardwood now, the music playing as I bounce the ball. My feet glide with confidence as I move downcourt. The ball bangs loudly, pressing against the floor with a mission. Before me runs the rat, scurrying down the court as fast as his hairy legs will move, his long tail dragging on the floor behind him. He looks back and sees the relentless look of the hunter. It is the first time One-on-One Willie has shown himself on the hardwood, wearing four legs. His pace increases at midcourt, and I speed up as well. At the three-point line, his body stretches out, front and back legs spread so far apart that the rat appears as if he is being pulled in half by a pair of opposing forces. The ball searches for his body, and I dribble with greater intensity the closer I get to him. He senses my closeness and moves back and forth erratically, trying to throw me off his trail. The ball bounces high and I palm it, driving it toward his body three feet below me. He jumps to the left and the ball bounces from the floor, narrowly missing him. He burrows beneath the safety of the bleachers, and I lunge Heavenward, executing a perfect, old school layup.

29

When silver doth glisten, a fool will listen.

He hasn't had air for a while, so I take him from the satchel. It is bright in the attic now, and I can see him fully for the first time. He certainly sleeps a lot, stretched out like that. I sit quietly, watching his body absorbing the light. I wrap my hand around him. He is quite warm. I study every detail of his head. His crown looks more royal in silver than it ever would in red, but I guess he got more accomplished as a crimson king. I rub the thorns.

"Did they even hurt by then, bro?" I whisper to him.

His eyes remain closed. He is his own little miracle. My fingers pass over his body, reading each imperfection like Braille.

"Did they?" I ask again.

I am thrown suddenly to the floor. I feel rough hands on me and hear the tearing of the garments from my body. I feel a sharp sting on my back, the pain so full of hatred it takes away my breath. I am frightened, for the robe is not mine.

The whippings? The beatings? The thorns piercing your skull? The slivers of the wooden cross gouging your back? The pounding of the nails? Did you even feel the lance blade plunging into your side by then? Did you? When is earthly pain no longer of significance? When does one stop feeling the hurt? Where lies the boundary between the physical and the spiritual? Between the living and the dead? Between body and soul?

I am almost jealous that he was whipped and I never was. For my cries come from blows barely struck, but his silence is testament to the cruel ones that were. And the real tragedy is that the biggest hurt never came from whip or club. It came from spit.

30

The attic warms and my eyes grow heavy from lack of sleep. I doze for a few moments, awakened by my own snoring. The knot on my head throbs, but I can feel that the swelling is going down. The cross lies across my lap, and I pick it up, studying it in the clear light. The metal appears to be coated with a thin, dull film. Curious, I begin to rub the body with the sleeve of my robe. The silver begins to shine. I rub harder, up and down the body of Christ. The light gleams off the fresh surface. I feel as if I have purged away the sins that tarnish a soul, and I feel a sense of satisfaction in my accomplishment. I bring the cross close to my face. My eyes find a blurry reflection in his thigh and are fascinated by what a curved universe can reveal. I see clearly the oversized blotches clogging my face. I press my finger against one.

"You could cure a leper, bro—but what 'bout me, huh? Why ain't you throwing some of that magic dust my way?"

I see my face, the blotches sinking beneath my skin, my face clear of blemish. I am pleased by what I see and I feel good. But he takes back his miracle and the blotches return, looming larger and more hideous than before.

A white robe of purity and trust stares back at me, but it masks the black of evil and betrayal. Mirrors, no matter what their shape, do not lie. I am a walking contradiction, and I have worked hard to remain so. No wonder the rat turned tail.

"Mrs. Foster?" I hear a voice call out in the hallway.

"Yes, Mrs. Lyons?" a second voice replied.

I look through the vent to see the pregnant lady speaking to the art teacher.

"Did you happen to see the crucifix from my art room wall? The one hanging on the wall? It's not there."

"No," the pregnant teacher replied, surprised. "I haven't seen it."

"It's missing," the art teacher said, "I wonder where it went."

"Perhaps Mrs. Withers borrowed it," the pregnant teacher suggested. "You know, for religion class."

"I'll ask her," the art teacher said. "It's a family heirloom. I certainly don't mind if she uses it, but it's strange that she didn't leave me a note or something. That's not like her."

"Maybe she meant to, but forgot," the pregnant lady replied. "You know how distracted she gets with all the different grades she teaches. When she gets excited about some new idea, she sometimes forgets just about everything."

"You're probably right," the art teacher agreed, grinning. "I won't even mention it to her. I wouldn't want to embarrass her. She'll tell me."

Right about then, that nice robe I was wearing wasn't feeling too white, but the black shirt was about the right color.

31

Nothing like a little music to lift a spirit.

I look down to the same music room that used to be mine. It has changed very little. A big room, it looks smaller than it is. All sorts of musical instruments are propped against its walls and spread haphazardly over shelves. A large set of drums occupies the left corner of the room, and next to it, a black piano. A tuba leans against another wall, as if merely dozing. A slide trombone stands rigidly near the center of the wall to my left, keeping company with a mammoth black case shaped like a guitar. Boxes are shoved against the walls and on shelves, I can see they are filled with sets of musical triangles, canastas, pint-sized cymbals, and those fantastic little hoops with the metal disks on the sides, the tambourine. All designed to make noise. Those notes come to me in the wake of the silence, each little dingle, clingle, clang, and twang, and my ears gratefully accept each sound, regardless of how harsh the memory.

On the walls hang several pictures of instruments, one of a sleek, black clarinet spewing purple smoke that spells out "JAZZ." A picture of Mozart, his face rather stodgy, stares out from the wall, as if the master is issuing a stern warning against the abuse of the scale. In the far right corner of the room, the music teacher sits waiting for her class in the tiniest desk I have ever seen. Its size makes her look like a giant, but adds precious space to the crowded room. The large, black piano sits to her right, making the desk appear even smaller, almost intimidated. She faces the doorway, and I sense she is anxious for her students to arrive. She taps a pencil on the surface of the desk as if playing a melody. Noises in the hallway tell her they are coming and a smile lights up her face as a young girl enters. Two boys follow closely behind her.

"Get ready for class quickly, children," the teacher says anxiously. "Let's not waste a moment. There is much to do today."

Soon the room is full. Students find their instruments and seat themselves on chairs arranged in four rows in the center of the room. The chairs face the piano. A bell rings, signaling the start of class.

Some things do not change over time. The violin player, handkerchief on her lap, sits at the end of the row, positioned so that she is unable to spear her fellow musicians. The trumpet players sit in the back row, their chairs pushed amply back from the students in the row in front of them. The smallest child in the room, a sickly boy with a sniffle, sits among a forest of drums. Clarinet players pipe softly, looking around as they warm up. A guitar player plucks the strings, fingers intent on tuning the instrument just right. He pauses for a moment to brush away a defiant lock of hair.

The teacher stands and moves to a seat in front of the piano keyboard. She waits patiently for the room to quiet, her conductor's stick in hand.

"Today, children, we will start class a little differently, with a bit of fun. Let's all raise our voices and sing a song to warm us up."

The sound of groaning sweeps through the room. She raps the stick sharply on the top of the piano. A wide crack opens where she struck and water gushes forward from the opening. Now that's somebody with connections.

"Hush, class," she admonishes as the flowing water ceases. "Did you expect that we'd be playing baseball? This is a music room. We learn music here."

She leafs through a songbook propped up in front of her. Finding the page she is seeking, her lips form a smile.

"Okay, class, you all know this song. It was written a very long time ago, in 1869, by a very nice man named Septimus Winner. You've all sung this when you were in the lower grades. It is called 'The Birdies' Ball.' It is a very light, fun song."

Her fingers dance on the piano keys, banging out the opening notes.

I know this song! We used to sing it in this very room!

"I'll sing the words," she says, "and you can warm your voices by singing the chorus."

She began, her shrill voice piercing the air above the crisp notes of the piano. The words reminded me of some old Irish tavern tune.

*Spring once said to the nightingale
I mean to give you birds a ball
Pray ma'am ask the birdies all
The birds and birdies great and small*

"Okay, class, come in on the beat. You know when."

Only a music teacher could sing a song this silly and make it sound as if there were some sense to it. The chorus is simple and anyone singing it couldn't help becoming at least a little merry. She points to her students and they begin, many young tongues poking out between lips as they sing.

*Tra la la la la
Tra la la la la
Tra la la la la
Tra la la la la
Tra la la la la
Tra la la la la
Tra la la la la la
Tra la la*

My tiny fingers gingerly hold a piece of white cord, and from it dangles my little metal triangle. It feels heavy but is not. My left hand holds a shiny steel rod about the size of a pencil. I stand stiffly on the stage, gazing out at an audience of parents. I am in the back row, on the highest of four steps. My music teacher is playing the song on a piano, singing the silly lyrics to one of the stanzas. I wait for the signal to bang on my triangle as she sings.

*Soon they came from bush and tree
Singing sweet their songs of glee
Each one fresh in its cozy nest
Each one dressed in its Sunday best*

She nods her head at me. When the *la* at the end of each line of the chorus is sung, I bang the metal rod against my triangle. I rap it sharply and crisply, as she has taught me to do. I stand as tall as my thirty-eight-inch body can, dressed in my tan school pants and white shirt with the "t" on the pocket. The audience is smiling. I sense they are all looking straight at me and at nobody else—in fact, I'm sure of it. Other than the teacher, I am the only one playing an instrument. When the last line of the chorus is sung, I rap my triangle three times in harmony with the *Tra la la.* The song ends with a furious storm of piano notes and me banging as hard as I can on my triangle. The audience explodes with applause. Mama is in the front row, smiling broadly as she claps. I look toward my music teacher. She bangs out a final chord and winks approvingly.

Below me, the teacher continues to sing another stanza and the children break into the chorus. A humming sound comes to my ears, not from below, but somewhere behind me in the rafters. I stand, following the noise. It leads me to a spot between two rafters. I stop to listen, my eyes finding that, for some reason, these two rafters are closer together than any of the others. At first, the sound appears to be a garbled humming, but as I listen, I realize that the humming is the resonation of the musical sounds below, transferred by some acoustic miracle through the wood of these magnificent rafters. I am standing between the prongs of a giant tuning fork. I put my hand on the wood and my fingers vibrate. The blood roof, it seems, sings as well.

Suddenly, the music is interrupted by the harsh sound of an alarm.

"Fire drill!" the music teacher shouts. "Everybody stand up!"

A clatter of noise as instruments are set down hard upon their respective chair seats. The teacher grabs a chart and glances at it. She surveys her class.

"Everyone out the door!" she commands. "And quickly. Line up on the sidewalk next to the playground. And no talking."

I watch them exit the room, the sweet notes of the piano still ringing in my ear. Above it the shrillness of the fire alarm has stirred up something else. And he is on the move.

32

They file from the building like lines of ants marching toward some picnic spread out before them, each anxious to take home a piece of the trophy. There are many lines, coming from many doors. The teachers walk along with them, and I peer through an opening, watching as each little head is counted. Finally, the school is completely emptied. The children are rounded up and shepherded to one location. One little girl points to a branch in a tree.

"Look!" she says. "It's Rory!"

As if aware that it has become the center of the attention, the squirrel flicks its tail. An excitement passes through the crowd as each student is quickly made aware of the presence of the squirrel.

A well-dressed woman stands on a small hill near the playground. She is distant from me, but I watch as her body and clothing transforms to that of the goat herder in the midst of the crowd. His voice is soft but easy to hear, his pet words being "Bles-sed be this" and "Bles-sed be that."

The well-dressed woman returns and puts a bullhorn to her mouth. She speaks.

"No talking in line, children. This is a fire drill and we need to do it right."

It is the same voice that opened the school day earlier. The principal.

I am amused. She preaches her sermon with a portable Way and Truth. As I think about how funny that is, I remember the speaker attached to the Other Wall near the Not-So-Fun Room. But then, I realize, *that* Way and Truth came later. The *original* Way and Truth *was* portable.

The voice speaks again.

"Very good, children. You evacuated the school in less than three minutes today. Very, very good. Next time, we'll do even better."

The children look around at each other, pleased by her words of praise.

"Teachers, kindly escort your students back inside now."

"Do we have to?" a very young voice asks. "Can't we stay out here and play?"

I can see the little boy, probably six years old. The principal looks down at him.

"Now, if we did that, Jimmy, we couldn't have any recess later, could we? And you wouldn't want to miss out on all that fun, would you?"

He nods his head grudgingly.

The teachers form lines, each class reentering the school in their turn. Mr. Devlin has also left the building, and the art teacher motions him over. They are right below me.

"Mr. Devlin," she begins, glancing toward the tree, "I think our little friend Rory has found a way into the attic again. I think I heard him running around up there earlier today."

The janitor looks toward the tree.

"In the attic?" he asks, concerned.

"Yes. We heard him."

"I will take care of it. Right now."

One can only hope that "right now" means tomorrow, in janitor time.

33

Each little head swings back and forth, up and down, and around and around. And I don't blame them. They are in the midst of an arithmetic test. They do the same things as we did back then. We gnawed on our pencils, too, as if sinking our teeth into the soft stem would force these writing utensils to surrender the correct answers hidden within the wood. And there's just something about biting off that tiny, pink eraser that seems as natural to do as not washing your hands before dinner. And chewing on that yummy metal band that holds the eraser in place is another great way of trying to dig those answers out from way inside.

The teacher walks through the aisle as the children take the test. Once in a while, a pupil looks up, rewarded by a smile of encouragement. She walks by one desk, where a frustrated student has rubbed a hole right through his test paper. He is biting on the pencil.

"Take it easy, Tommy," she says. "Slow down and take your time. I'm sure you know this material." She taps his head. "And what's more important is for you to know that it's right in there."

Her hand brushes across the surface of his desk, sweeping the eraser shavings over the side. She crouches eye level with him, looking at his answers.

"You're doing fine so far, Tommy. I can tell. Now keep it up."

She pats him on the back and stands, continuing down the aisle. I can feel the warmth of her hand fading from my back and my nose detects a sweet perfume of days gone by.

A tremendous cracking sound erupts in the air, racing down the rafters and into the distant parts of the attic. A blinding light from below floods the far corner of the attic. My heart pounds and blood rushes through my brain. Someone has ripped open the Big White. If they ascend, I will surely be discovered. If my dark face could blanch, it just did.

Roosters crow in many colors, but High Priests of Black and White know only one. Betrayal. Confinement. Denial. Denial. Denial. And then—

Please, Lord, not again.

Cock-a-doodle-doo!

I hear the sole of a shoe grind against the Stairway to Heaven, followed by a second. Adrenaline pumps through me as a head pokes into the attic. The white robe will expose me, but if I attempt to take it off now, my motions will be seen. I duck behind a rafter, crouching low. It is Mr. Devlin's head, rising from below. He emerges into the attic, the strong springs on the Big White closing the opening behind him. He picks his way along the board path he seems familiar with. He carries a cane, and the rhythm of the slow, dull thuds comes to my ears. He pokes at the boards of the catwalk as he limps into the faint light beneath the rafters. He stops for a moment, resting a free hand against his chest, his breathing labored. My senses tell me that the man has already made up his mind where he is going. I attempt to deflate myself, to make my body as small as possible, and he doesn't seem to notice me. He walks to the stack of boxes and around them, to the manger scene. He lowers his head and stares down for a very long time. He leans over, supporting his weight on his cane, and picks up the baby Jesus. He studies it for a while, then talks to it.

"Kinda cold outside then, wasn't it, little fella? Hope it's a little warmer for you up here."

He strokes the tiny figurine against his cheek and holds it tightly there for a moment. In a small corner of a cold world, this man of wasting body bestows a declining warmth upon his champion. He has searched beyond the plaster and found the prize. My eyes begin to tear—I cannot help it. I am witnessing something too deep for words. I feel ashamed and cannot understand why. Is it because I stand witness to the depth of his faith, or because I concede the shallowness of my own?

He holds the little statue in his hand for a moment longer and returns it to the parents. His eyes fall upon another object. He grunts and picks it up. It is the Wise Man holding the frankincense. He studies it, shaking his head as his rough finger moves across the marred bottle in the statue's hand.

"Rory, Rory, Rory," he says, looking around. "What am I going to do with you, little guy?"

He leans forward and puts the figure back. He hobbles toward the spot above the art room. I am a statue as he walks right by my rafter. He doesn't see me and I cannot understand why. But my whole being aches to spring up like a morning flower facing the dawn and shout to him, "Mr. Devlin, it's me! It's Bitsy! I'm here!" And see him smile when he recognizes my face. But then, that Bitsy's long gone, and we both know it.

I can feel the sack of Jesus swinging against my thigh. Perhaps there is purpose in this man's blindness. His cane reaches out to the shadows. I hear the hard snap of a trap being sprung.

"Can't have you being hurt, little squirrel friend," he says to the rafters. "But you ornery varmint, cut your teeth somewhere other than in my stable."

Once again, blame has been heaped upon the innocent.

He descends the Stairway to Heaven. The springs of the Big White creak shut, protesting as they do so.

34

It is quiet beneath the rafters, and in this isolation, strange thoughts come. I glance at the sleeper on the cross. I look at the dark skin covering my arm and wonder about his color. Was he darker than white? Or was whiter than dark? Is my blood redder than his because my skin is darker? Does it matter? Maybe that's why, of all the people who knew him, who wrote about him, not one person ever said what he looked like. Not one. With a message like his, perhaps it just didn't matter. Other things about him held their attention. I chuckle, trying to imagine him with blotches of freckles and curly, yellow hair, but his face will not come to me, only the faces others have drawn. My fingers flex open and close, and I hold my hand high, marveling at the wonder of this body that has been gifted to me. For a moment, a hole opens in my palm and I can see through my hand. What patiently waits through the opening amazes me.

He also had a body, was a body. All the things this magnificent machine can do. With all my gripes about my color, it is a wonder of nature, even with the freckles and yellow hair. Why is it that this man creature is so hung up on skin? Why is he so destined to fight over it? To kill for it? It doesn't matter really, if it's the skin of a man or the skin of a mink. Sooner or later, there's a fight coming. And shame on us all for it.

I hear the murmur of voices and rise, picking my footsteps, gingerly moving over the board path below the rafters. My hands find balance on the massive wooden beams and my fingertips feel an impression in the wood. I stop to examine it. Someone has carved words deep into the rafter, the letters crossing the grain at right angles. My eyes focus, making out the writing.

Johnny F. and Freddie D. fired up a Camel 5/25

I grin as I read these words.

Well, isn't this a fine howdy do? My mind sees them opening the Big White and climbing the Stairway to Heaven, snickering all the while. Up here, where their deeds go unseen, they light a cigarette and forge a bond with their sin. Not really a sin, I guess. Let's just say a sneaky prank. Stupid, but sneaky. I'm willing to bet a dime to a dollar that these were eighth-graders about to graduate, 'cause it's May when they did it, and this has the smell of older kids. They roam more freely around the school than do younger ones. Wonder what these fine *Chris-ti-an* boys, *Johnny F. and Freddie D.*, are up to these days. Wonder where all this goody two-shoe talk they learned here has gotten them. Further than me, I would imagine.

My fingers trace their message and I move on, following the rising murmur to the lunchroom.

I kneel down, staring through the vent ridges at table after table of students, each child with a lunch spread out before them. My mouth waters and my stomach growls, as through the squares in the vent, I see rows of apples, sandwiches, cookies, potato chips, and candies and baked treats in the shape of red hearts. It is February, I remind myself. And sitting among all that food are pint-sized cartons of milk, looking the same as they did when I sat at these tables. Wonder if they're more than two cents now. What I wouldn't give for a carton of milk, don't matter much right now if it's white or chocolate. The scene is the same all over the lunchroom, with tables filled with little children mixed with tables of bigger kids, each table with eight lunches just beyond my reach.

I sit among my friends in the lunchroom and we are all laughing. White milk drools over my lip as I laugh, my open mouth stuffed with one of mama's chocolate cookies. She could make a mean cookie, that's for sure. The fun times in the lunchroom. It's not fair to be so close and yet so far.

I look down at my sack of Jesus.

"You lucky you're made of silver, bro. You never get to go hungry."

Silver stirs a hunger down deep, that's for sure. But nothing's bad as what it is. What's bad is how it's used.

I see something moving and my eyes turn from the vent. I squint and see the long tail of the rat. The rodent is making his way to the stable. I see the baby lying in the manger, still as stone. The rat is picking his way among the statues, each figure frozen in fear. His long whiskers brush past the tiny camels and dogs and shepherds, looming eyes fixed on the manger.

I gasp, shaking the image from my head.

The rat continues toward the stack of boxes rising before him, the stable shivering next to them. The tall stack transforms into the hospital, and next to it, the liquor store that imprisons my loaves and fishes. It dawns on me that I am not all that different from the rat, and this revelation stuns me. Creature of the night. Thief from the black river.

My feet tiptoe along the boards of the catwalk as I follow. His tail weaves a dust trail in the floor. He stops before the stable, sensing my presence behind him. He rises on his hind legs and pulls himself over the roof of the stable. The baby Jesus sleeps directly below him.

I see Mr. Devlin. He stands before the stable, holding the little baby. The child's face has been gnawed away. Mr. Fix It is weeping.

35

My foot stomps hard on the catwalk and I regret my action immediately. The rat flees into the darkness and I wait in silence for some sign of detection from below. I hear nothing and I am grateful no one has heard me. I turn to make my way back to the lunchroom. My anger at the rat grows and I hold the sack of Jesus in one hand, jamming the other into the opposite pocket of my robe. My fingers bump against something deep in the pocket.

I do not know miracles, but I know of them.

The robe has been warming my body for hours, and in all that time, I hadn't felt the presence of the bulge. But it is there now. My fingers surround the object and pull it from its hiding place. It crinkles. I hold it up, stunned.

"Well, I'll be—"

It's a Baby Ruth bar, the wrapper looking as new as if it had just come from the candy factory. Hasn't even been stepped on. The paper feels cool. My hunger burns but my mind is confused. I look down at my sack of Jesus, but he gives me no clue.

Anxious fingers tear open the wrapper, and the sweet aroma of chocolate comes to me, fueling my hunger. I take a big bite and chew the candy, the chocolate mixing with peanuts in my mouth. This must be Heaven and I am the Taster Angel. A second bite tastes just as sweet as the engine in my stomach roars to life. As I chew, I crave white milk, but know that this gift is more than I had and surely much more than I deserve.

A miracle must be believed, like the sound of a tree falling in the forest when no one's listening. In some not-so-distant past, a boy in a choir reached into his pocket between songs of a Christmas program. He is distracted and pulls his hand out before achieving his goal. Whoever wore the gold-cuffed robe before me returned it to the box in a hurry, forgetting his prize. And that is miracle enough for right now.

36

I save the last bite, placing the fat morsel back into its wrapper and returning it to my pocket. I have had my lunch and the students have had theirs. Through spaces in the fascia boards, I watch them outside at recess, laughing and horse playing. A boy swings on the monkey bars, and I wonder how long I could hang there. Used to could hang there forever. A group of girls play dodgeball until two boys steal away the ball. Bitsy was the one they used to shove through the little hole in the wire to get the ball back when it sailed over the fence back then. Another girl is twirling a hula hoop, and how she's keeping it going is beyond me. I never could get past two seconds with that thing, but I could sure hang on the monkey bars. Monkey Man at his finest. On a piece of grass in the far corner of the playground, a football spirals clumsily through the air.

The mule is on the run, cradling the football beneath an arm, charging down the open field. A few daring boys stand before me, but I cut to the right and then, just as quickly, back left. I am the fastest one on the field and they know it. It doesn't hurt to be the most stubborn, either. I score one more time and my teammates sing as my feet cross the goal line.

Itsy Bitsy spider gets us one more goal
No one can catch him 'cause he has got the soul
If you ever bring him down you are pretty neat
For the Itsy Bitsy spider has got the fastest feet

I am the king of the gridiron and master of the hardwood. And life is good.

Funny, nobody's ever called me "the word" during my whole life. That's something I'd remember. Probably 'cause my hair's yellow and people can't quite figure out what to make of me. Don't know what to call me. But they looked it. I surely know they looked it. But no one ever gave me that look here. I had forgotten that the things they called me here in Jesusville were all good.

37

Attics always seem to have this stale smell. I should know—I've spent a lot of time in attics. It is the smell of dried old and this attic is no different. And the smell seems to grow stronger as the sun heats the roof. But the heat feels good, warming my robe. The smell of the sewer drifts through occasionally as shifting breezes carry vent gases from above the roof back through cracks in the boards. Luckily, though, the breezes change direction, and the smell does not linger.

Sometimes, stink doesn't even have a smell. On all the forms she ever wrote out for me, mama filled them in when the donkey wasn't around. She checked off "Black" so he wouldn't know. As if hiding the truth behind a penciled "X" would cleanse away the white poison she saw and let me be protected by the dark. It was only later, after mama died, that I began "X"ing in "Other." But an "X" there did about as much good as do eyes to a blind man. Nobody sees "Other."

Jesus looks up at me and I wonder if he knows what I'm thinking. His eyes are seeking. I feel I must say something.

"Maybe your daddy sent the wrong son, too, bro," I blurt out. "You suppose that was the deal?"

I regret my words immediately and cover my mouth with a hand. I glance toward the rafters, cringing in anticipation of a lightning bolt. I pick up the cross, staring into the face.

"Sorry I said that, bro, truly I am. It's not altogether your fault that things turned out the way they did."

Of course, who am I to be preaching anything to anyone? Here I am, raised to be God-fearing, but choosing instead to be a thief. I'm hiding in an attic with a rat, wearing a white robe with a half-eaten Baby Ruth in the pocket and talking to a glob of silver. I am the Lord of the Rafters and this is my kingdom. I take a deep breath and look around. But tomorrow will come, and all of this will be gone and forgotten. My eyes meet his.

"I ain't asking for that much, am I, bro? I just want to live on my side of the street. You can keep your side the way you like and I promise I won't bother you."

I stare at him.

"Give to Bitsy what is Bitsy's then, bro. And to you, what be yours."

It dawns on me that the words I have just uttered are his, spoken to reaffirm his acknowledgement of a great ruler. But in my white robe with gold fringe, dust dancing in the air of my tiny kingdom, I am a pathetic Caesar.

38

He is back. I hear his body swishing against the stack of boxes as he makes his way to the manger scene once more. His head pokes out from between two boxes. Coarse whiskers twitch as his cold, bottomless eyes meet mine. A long, gray tail laces like a snake around the corner of the box. His nose has picked up the scent of chocolate and he is curious. I do not know when he last ate, and as he stares at me with wicked eyes, a sense of fright overcomes me. I see the chewed-up face of the baby in the manger and a shiver runs down my spine. He will go to the stable again—I know he will. I cannot allow him to do that. He turns his head and his eyes shine with an evil red set against a dark, gray head. His whiskers twitch again, and in the shadows, I see his demon form, rising up to challenge the mule. Perhaps he will come for me first. To steal, as thieves do. My body shakes. Is this how they feel about me?

His eyes are fixed, glowing like coals, and I know my presence does not frighten him. My skin pricks, feeling the very presence of the devil himself with me beneath these rafters. I wonder why God just didn't eliminate that horrible creature if His Almighty truly packs that much heat. He created this evil and brought it the world, after all. Couldn't he kill him? Why doesn't he just take him out to remove *all* evil from the world? Can't he break his own commandments? Who would know anyway? Who would dare hold him accountable? And who would blame him? Can he kill? My mind shuts down for an instant as an eerie thought passes through. Could *I* kill the devil if I had the chance? If I had his power for just one moment, would I take this evil out? He is also a creature made of and by him. It is an intriguing paradox, the killing of a devil.

The rat continues to stare at me. With his vile appearance, I know he is an extension of the Prince of Darkness. I wonder if this vermin runs rabid, and my thoughts turn to all the children in the classrooms below me. What if he is hungry as well? I hear voices below me. What if he finds a way down there and gets loose among the children? I see a screaming girl in a crowded lunchroom, furiously shaking a hideous ball of fur from her arm as classmates watch, horrified. Blood drips from an open wound as the menace buries its teeth deeper into her tender flesh, and the girl shakes her arm even harder. She screams horrifically in pain, terrified at this hairy growth clutching her. They all shriek, unable to comprehend why evil is here, in their Jesus school. The rat releases his grip and inches up her arm to gnaw away her face.

If I could kill the devil, then I am bound by honor to kill his child. I glance down at the sleeping face in my sack, but need no approval. His will be done.

39

He scurries away as I rise, his body shrinking as he distances himself from me. I shove the crucifix deep into my satchel, making sure the cloth hides his head. My footsteps backtrack to a spot where Mr. Devlin has just been and I find the sprung trap. Picking it up, I detect the rancid scent of old death. The trap has held stilled flesh before. I walk to the manger and sit down on one of the boxes. I am uncertain as to what I am about to do, but I continue. I place the trap on top of a box and bring the remains of the candy bar forth from my pocket. The aroma of the chocolate is still sweet and strong. I long for the final bite, but fight the urge. I know the devil's child cannot resist this temptation any more than I can.

My eyes reach out into the depths of the rafters and I know he is watching me. The trap is heavy and the hard, copper-colored coils wait in anticipation. The death stench stirs as I lift up the bait tongue. If the devil's child is smart enough to find his way up here, perhaps he is smart enough to steal the bait without setting off the trap. He is a thief, after all, one not to underestimate.

I remove the candy from the wrapper and roll a small piece between my fingers to soften the chocolate. When the candy is warm enough, I reshape it into a round blob and set it on the box next to me. I pick up the trap and pull back on the rectangular death wire, and as I do so, I feel the copper-colored coils tense. I lift the death wire up and over the coils to the opposite end of the wooden base, and I can feel the stored energy yearning to spring free. I pull the long shank of wire over the death wire to hold it down and place the end of the shank in the notch of the bait tongue. I lift the bait tongue up, locking the long shank in place, the tension holding back the death wire.

I pick up the brown blob, sensing irony that the rat's last supper will go unconsumed. The chocolate smell tempts me as I ease the candy beneath the bait tongue. A smart rat would pick the bait tongue clean, leaving the trap unsprung, but any rodent trying to steal food wedged under the tongue will be more likely to set off the trap. I will not be here in the rafters forever. I have only one chance at killing the devil's child.

As my black fingers work with the trap, the thought comes that the evil I hunt is just as dark as me, maybe darker. And he steals, like me. So much for honor among thieves. I am a creature of darkness and I am killing one of my own.

Thank God I got Jesus hidden away in the sack.

40

I lick my fingers, cleaning away smears of chocolate. My eyes study the trap for a few moments, as if unsure, but cautious hands gently pick it up. My feet move slowly around the boxes to the stable where I know he will come. I place the trap next to the manger and step away, but I do not like what I see—death at the birthplace. That is not supposed to happen. Death will come soon enough. I move the trap just outside the stable scene and back away. It is an odd paradox, a trap beckoning eternal death next to a manger offering eternal life. But what's done is done, and I feel better for it.

I look down to the manger one last time before I turn away and a strange thought comes to me. Manger Boy is a half-breed, just like me. Half of Heaven and half of Earth. The ultimate one-drop rule. And here I am, soaking in my sorry sauce, thinking the mule had the load to carry. Ain't that a hoot? I ain't been carrying but one body on my back. He had to carry them all.

I peer through some of the vents as I move about. Students trying to figure out answers, always up against some concept they have yet to grasp. The pregnant teacher continues to teach, still uncomfortable with her clumsy belly.

"Okay, class," she says. "It's time for spelling. Take out your books."

With much fanfare, they switch books, opening to the page of interest. She motions to one student.

"Martha, can you spell 'excitement?'"

A young girl with long, brown hair stands up. Clasping her hands together, she thinks and takes a deep breath.

"E-x-c-i-t-e-m-e-n-t—excitement."

"Very good," the teacher answers, looking around. "Now, Bitsy, can you give us a word to spell?"

My heart swells.

"I've got a word," I reply proudly.

And I say that word for the class, nice and loud.

"That's so easy," a girl's voice answers.

"Okay, Mary," the teacher instructs, "spell it."
The girl rises.
"F-o-e—foe," she replies. "It means opponent. Child's play."
She sits down, acting like I was wasting her valuable time.
"Is she correct in her spelling, Bitsy?" the teacher asks.
"No," I answer. "That's not right at all."
The teacher looks puzzled.
"Are you sure about that, Bitsy?"
"Oh, I'm sure 'bout that, ma'am."
"Okay, Bitsy, then why don't you spell 'foe' for the class?"
My chest swells and I do as she asks.
"F-o-u-r."

The class howls in laughter, and I follow their lead for some reason I do not know. So don't be talking to me 'bout no lost sheep needing saving while the rest sit safely in pasture.

41

The bell rings and I am standing above another classroom, staring down at the tops of many little heads. Lots of colors down there. A boy sits fidgeting, his flaming red hair trimmed in a crew cut. Several other boys have blond hair, clean-looking, quite different from the dirty mop of uncertainty I got stuck with. A fat boy sits in his cramped desk, his hair, thick and black, sheltering the top of his ears. It shines up at me like a black sun, and the reflection moves whenever he turns his head. The predominant hair color among the boys is brown, and many shades of it.

The girls have more variety in their hair, not only in color but also by how they wear it. Half a dozen of them sport ponytails and one has a wild-looking whale spout. The hair of a pretty, fair-skinned blond is adorned with dozens of large curls, and buried in this nest of curls is a pink butterfly barrette. A black girl wears cornrows decorated with multicolor beads that clack when her head moves, and a sleepy-eyed Oriental girl wears short hair that curves inward to her neck.

I look down to my sack of Jesus.

"Is this how your daddy sees it all, bro? Looking down at tops of heads all day?" I grin. "Maybe some days, that might be all he wants to see."

He doesn't reply.

I see it in the rafters—the absolute grandeur of the symmetry surrounding me. There is beauty in structure, in substance, and in color. There is beauty in purple. There is beauty in red. And maybe somewhere there is beauty in black. I speak to him.

"But you don't care about beauty at all, do you, bro? Beautiful and ugly are the same to you. Maybe that's what your beauty is about—what makes it work. Why you're still around."

"Okay, class," the teacher begins. "Who can tell me what special day is coming up this month?"

Every hand in the room shoots up. She points to one of them.

"Jenny, can you tell us?"

"Yes, Mrs. Withers."

Mrs. Withers? Where have I heard that name before? Oh, yes, didn't you pinch the cross from the art room wall? Naughty, naughty, Mrs. Withers. And you, the religion teacher.

"It's Valentine's Day," the young girl answers enthusiastically.

The room is filled with giggles.

"That's right," Mrs. Withers answers. "Valentine's Day. And we celebrate Valentine's Day by remembering those we love."

A few heads turn, and anxious glances are thrown back and forth. There are giggles all over.

"But it is also an excellent time to get to know someone who you maybe don't like so much. Maybe someone has done something to you that wasn't so nice. Or maybe you think they did, or maybe someone told you they did, but you really don't know if it's true or not. Or maybe you don't like someone, but you really don't know why you don't like them because you've never gotten to know them."

I feel warm now as I kneel in the darkness, listening. The robe has served its purpose and I momentarily ponder discarding the garment, but change my mind. My kingdom is of this world and the robe speaks as the symbol of my office.

"There are a lot of themes that we can address at Valentine's Day," Mrs. Withers explains. "Now, does anyone remember the story of the Good Samaritan?"

Several hands shoot up. Mrs. Withers waves them down.

"That's good that you remember, class. The story of the Good Samaritan is a great lesson on why we should help a person who needs it even though old prejudices tell us not to."

She points to a boy.

"Timmy, tell us about the Good Samaritan, please."

"This guy was walking down the road," the boy begins, "minding his own business, and a couple of guys rob him and beat him up. Then they leave him there in the middle of the road, bleeding and everything."

Mrs. Withers smiles.

"Very good, Timmy. Now, who can tell us what happened next?"

She points to a girl waving her hand frantically.

"Okay, Margaret, for heaven's sake, tell us before your arm flies off."

She speaks.

"Then this guy comes down the road and finds him, but just keeps going. And then this other guy wearing Levis does the same thing."

Mrs. Wither chuckles.

"Well, I don't know if he was wearing Levis, Margaret, but he was a Levite, and he didn't stop to help the man, either, just like the first traveler didn't stop."

She looks around the room.

"Why don't you suppose they didn't stop to help this injured man, class?"

The class hesitates, whispering to each other.

"They were in a hurry?" one boy offers.

"Maybe they thought he was a bum, sleeping it off," another boy says.

"They didn't know him?" another asks.

"They were afraid of the robbers?" a fourth suggests.

"Good answers, children," Mrs. Withers says. "All good answers and all possibly are correct. Any of those could be the answer. But didn't Jesus tell us that greater love hath no man than one who would lay down his life for another? In this case, they didn't have to do that. All they had to do was stop. Do you think these two men should have stopped to help—maybe just to offer a drink of water?"

The class nodded their heads in agreement.

"Who do you think committed the greater crime?" she asks. "The men who beat and robbed this man or the men who failed to come to his aid?"

A tiny girl raises her hand.

"Yes, Julie?" Mrs. Withers says.

"The men who left him by the road," the girl answers.

"Why?"

The girl hesitates.

"Because," she stammers, "just because."

"Good answer, Julie," Mrs. Withers smiles. "Sometimes, we can't explain why—and that's okay—we just know what the right thing to do is. Some people who think they are great intellects might try to justify the actions of these men—that it's okay not to render aid to those in need. They talk themselves right into a false sense of right—but it's a lie. And our history books are filled with examples of times when humans mistreated other humans and the rest of the world stood by and let it happen."

"So what happened to the men who walked on by?" Margaret asks.

"I guess we'll never know," Mrs. Withers replies. "Not on this earth anyhow. It's up to someone other than us to answer that question, and he probably rendered judgment on those men a long time ago."

I am always perplexed when I think about that "being taken care of" part. If God truly loves someone that much, how could he send them to hell? Shoot them down in a ball of flames. I couldn't do it. I couldn't send my own sons or daughters—my own flesh and blood—to a place like hell. I couldn't let them be in a place like that, no matter how bad they'd been. Someday, I might even have my own son, and the thought of him burning in flames as the end result of his earthly existence horrifies me. To dwell in a fire that does not die, to suffer a pain that has no end. How does one earn an eternal punishment for a finite misdeed? It doesn't seem fair.

Jesus is bouncing a basketball now as we walk side by side down the hardwood. He looks downcourt, smiling, and passes the ball my way without looking.

But I ain't him and the rules are his, not mine.

"So, what finally happened to the man who was beaten?" Mrs. Wither asks.

"He was saved," a voice pipes in triumphantly, "by the Good Samaritan."

"That is correct," Mrs. Withers replies. "The Good Samaritan happened by and took care of the man's wounds, and carried him to an inn and paid for his room until he got better. And what is significant here is that the man who helped him was from Samaria, and people from Samaria were looked down upon at that time."

"Why was that?" a voice asks.

"Old prejudices," Mrs. Wither answers. "Remember how I said that sometimes we don't understand other people, but don't really try to, either? Many people who read the Bible today don't know that the people of Samaria were of mixed race—"

My eyes widen.

"—descendants of intermarriage between Israelites and Assyrians, and they were looked down upon by other people because of this."

An arm of the crucifix pokes my side and I look down at him.

"You trying to escape things, too, ain't ya, bro? I wouldn't hang around with these purebreds if I didn't have to, either. Hate's just running around rampant and the time and place don't seem to matter much. But you got to go home to your daddy, didn't you, bro? I don't blame you for that. But I can't outrun the donkey. Never could and never will."

"So you see, class," Mrs. Withers continues, "you learned a little something today. Would you ever have thought that Valentine's Day had anything to do with the Good Samaritan?"

42

They are between classes now and I peer down into another room. This one is filled with pictures of people, a lot of whom are black. That's right—February is Black History Month. I see a picture of Martin Luther King Jr. hanging on the wall. I lean down, my face close to the vent. His expression looks serious from where I am, but he could be smiling. I see a picture of two black athletes on separate podiums, each raising an arm in the air, and I remember seeing this picture before. And that looks like Thurgood Marshall hanging on the wall beside them. There is a picture of some blacks working in a cotton field, all bunched over as they toil. There are other pictures all over the walls, all showing something historical about blacks.

As I look at the pictures below, my finger traces a path in the dust coating a board on the catwalk. I write "Bitsy" in the dust, my handwriting barely legible. Used to be that I was a good writer, 'til the donkey went away. Then I found out I got a lot more attention if I wrote badly, so I did. Then bad writing started to come to me naturally, becoming a friend I could have done without.

I watch specks of dust flickering in the air, the light bouncing from them like little mirrors. Remember, man, that thou art dust, and to dust thou shall return. Yeah, I remember that part. Like it means anything.

I look down at the letters I have written. My finger drops down to a spot just below them, where more dust lies in an undisturbed film. I stare at the blankness and my finger begins to move across the board, stopping when "Bitsy" is written once more. I pull my finger. The handwriting is beautiful, shaming the coarse letters above it. A book crashes hard to the floor in the classroom below and I hurriedly wipe away the letters that betray my other self.

The children begin to enter the classroom, bringing with them all the noise they can carry. The teacher motions for silence as the students find their seats.

"Good afternoon, class," the teacher greets.

"Good afternoon, Mrs. Pickett," they answer.

"We have been studying famous black people in our social studies class, students," she begins, "since this is Black History Month. We've studied about great statesmen and scientists, men and women of color who have contributed to the benefit of mankind. We have learned of the great deeds of black pioneers, particularly athletes, who have broken the color barrier in sports such as baseball, basketball, and even golf. And as the month goes by, we will study about more of them. In fact, tomorrow, we will learn about the Tuskegee Airmen who were the first black fighter pilots of World War II, and whose actions in combat distinguished these men during that war."

She pauses.

"But today, we will do a little something different. Can anyone tell me what the word 'Mulatto' means?"

My ears perk. Mulatto? Nobody talks about Mulattoes, lady. Ain't no such thing as Half-A-Black History Month, don't ya know?

She looks around, but no hands are raised to reply.

"Nobody?" she says. "I thought not."

She pulls something from behind her back and raises it up to the class. It is a figure she has made from two pieces of construction paper. The left side of the body is black and the right side is white.

"Mulatto is a type of race," she explains.

We're a race all right—we're always racing to get there and everybody else is racing to get away.

"I have constructed this simple figure to show you what a Mulatto is. A Mulatto is a person whose one parent is black and whose other parent is white." She shakes the paper figure. "Now this is a very simplistic way of showing you—it's actually more complicated than the paper I hold—but it is the easiest way I could think of to demonstrate the concept to you."

Complicated, ya think? You want complicated? Step into my office, sister, and I will show you complicated.

"Does everyone understand?"

Understand? Are you kiddin' me, lady? Wait a minute—why are they talking about half-breeds, today of all days? What are the chances of that? My eyes lift to the rafters, eyebrows cocked.

"That you up there, settin' me up, Big Daddy?"

I look at the cross.

"Or is it you, bro?"

And I thought the candy bar was a miracle.

Mrs. Pickett holds up a large photograph of young woman of dark skin, not too dark, though. Even from a distance, I can see her beauty.

"Now, this pretty lady is Dorothy Dandridge, class," Mrs. Pickett explains. "She was one of the first Mulatto celebrities and a movie star. She starred in movies at a time when people of color weren't allowed to star in motion pictures. But she was so talented and so beautiful that people looked beyond her dark skin and saw her for what she was. She was a true pioneer in the motion picture industry, opening the door for others to follow."

The teacher sets the picture aside and picks up a second photo.

"Does anyone know who this is?" she asks.

"I know!" a boy shouts from the back of the room. "That's Catwoman!"

"Right you are, Joey," she says. "This woman is an actress named Halle Berry, and she's a popular movie star today. You can see how pretty she is. She is also of the Mulatto race."

Halle Berry a Mulatto? I didn't know that. I rub my chin. Now, about that no messing with the womenfolk commandment, Big Daddy—I might have to rethink that one a bit.

"So I'm bringing to your attention, class, the fact that the Mulatto race has also made many contributions to mankind. The great writer and orator, Frederick Douglas, was not actually black, as most people associate him, but he was of the Mulatto race."

She turns to her desk, putting the photo down. She turns back, holding another photo, but keeping the picture from the class.

"One of the problems with being of mixed race, class," she explains, "is one of feeling alienated from everybody. How would you feel if one of your parents was black and the other was white?"

A hand rises up shyly, looking like a slow-growing orchid.

"Margaret?"

"I guess I'd wonder where I belonged, Mrs. Pickett."

"Did you hear Margaret's answer, class? She wonders about how mixed race kids feel about themselves. Why would that even be a concern, Margaret?"

"Oh, Mrs. Pickett," the girl answers. "It wouldn't make any difference to me. Not a bit. But it might to others."

The teacher smiles.

"Would that the world had your heart, Margaret."

Mrs. Pickett turns the photo over. It is a face of a black man with a mustache. The man wears a suit and his hair is funny, slicked back with oil and looking like melted butter smeared all over his head. I look closer. He doesn't exactly look like a black man. His face looks kind of white, as a matter of fact. And he looks familiar for some reason.

"This is a picture of a man who wrote about his dilemma of being of mixed race," Mrs. Pickett explains. "His name was Langston Hughes and he was a great Mulatto writer and poet."

My eyes widen. My hand shoots to muffle words wanting to burst from my mouth. For I was not born Bitsy. Mama gave me my Christian name—Langston Pittman—Langston Hughes Pittman. I am stunned. There is no coincidence here.

"We don't understand the thoughts or feelings that a person of mixed race would experience, class. But Langston Hughes did. He was a Mulatto, and he said so in his writings, that he was part white, part black, and even part Indian. And he wrote about the dilemma of not truly belonging to any race. In writings found after his death, a poem titled 'My Left Side Right Side' was discovered, and may have been written by him late in his life, but never published."

I look down to the crucifix on my hip.

"What is going on here, bro?"

"I'm going to read it to you, class. It is very short, but says a lot about why people of mixed race sometimes feel they don't fit in anywhere."

She picks up a paper from the desk, holding it in front of her as she keeps the photo up as well.

"My Left Side Right Side," she says, "by Langston Hughes."

She holds the man's photo out to the class.

One side of me is left
One side of me is right
And neither is the other
One conceals a shadow
One glows in white
One side lives in night's moonbeams
But can't be told
One basks in the sunlight
And though breathtaking, dares not be known
A work of art 'cause the paint don't mix
Side by side they ride
One constrained, one wishing he were so
Free to run, but wired, the beast can only roam

They always pull the skeletons from the closet, cutting off the good flesh first. I remember now. The picture on the wall of mama's house, right across the room from the goat herder. It was his photo hanging there—this man right here. And I remember there was some writing at the bottom of the picture. But I doubt if my God-fearing mama, in her hero worship of him, ever figured out that his box was checked "Other."

43

I see his photo before me again, his face hauntingly clear.

"When Langston Hughes visited Africa," Mrs. Pickett tells the class, "the native Africans told him something that shocked him. They told him he wasn't a black man and that really surprised him. His skin was black enough, but his blood wasn't. He wasn't a black man in Africa, but he was in America."

Ain't that a kick? The one-drop rule going the other way. Now that doesn't happen every day.

I'm seated in the front desk, watching several of my fellow third-graders standing before the class. We are doing Blink and Spin. Mrs. Dodgen hands a donut to one of three students clustered before the class. A boy stands away from the group, his back to them. He cannot see what Mrs. Dodgen has given the student.

"Ok, Timmy," she says to the lone student, "turn around and open and shut your eyes quickly as you are going around. And if you're too slow, you're out."

Timmy Butler spins around, opens his eyes in a flash, and continues to spin until his back is to the cluster once more.

"Who is holding the prize?" Mrs. Dodgen asks.

"Elaine," Timmy replies gleefully. "Elaine is holding a donut."

Mrs. Dodgen selects Betty Craven to replace Timmy and repeats the Blink and Spin, this time using a turnip. Betty misses it, seeing an onion as she spins around. The next two students correctly guess a stapler and a plastic palm tree.

We normally play only one game each week, but to our surprise, Mrs. Dodgen switches games, something she has never done before.

"We have some extra time today," she explains. "So why don't we play 'Guess Who?'"

During this game, one student is blindfolded and stands before the class, and a second student is brought before the first. The blindfolded student asks three questions and then has to guess who the mystery student is based on the answers. Mrs. Dodgen blindfolds

Buddy Armstrong and motions for Eddie Merkle up to get up and stand before him.

"Start guessing, Buddy," she instructs.

"Is it a boy?" Buddy asks.

"Yes," Mrs. Dodgen answers. "You are correct."

"Does he have blond hair?"

"Yes," she answers. "A blond boy. Good guess, Buddy."

"Now, last question," she says.

Buddy sniffs the air.

"Does he have freckles?" he asks

"Yes," Mrs. Dodgen replies. "Lots of freckles. Care to guess who it is, Mr. Armstrong?"

"It's Eddie Merkle," Buddy grins. "And I can smell his hair oil from here."

The class erupts in laughter. Mrs. Dodgen brings two more sets of students up to the front of the room, and each of the blindfolded students guesses incorrectly about the mystery person's identity. She motions to Billy Cantrell, the notorious class bully. He's mean to most of the kids, me in particular, but I can outrun him. Mrs. Dodgen blindfolds Billy and motions for me to stand before him, a finger pressed to her lips.

"Come here, Margaret Conner," she whispers so Billy can hear.

The whole class knows Billy is sweet on Margaret. But it's not Margaret Conner standing before Billy—it's me.

"Ok, Billy," Mrs. Dodgen instructs, "ask away."

"Is this myster-i-ous person smart?" Billy asks coyly.

The class grins.

"Quite smart," Mrs. Dodgen replies.

"Is this myster-i-ous person pretty?"

"Quite handsome, in fact," Mrs. Dodgen answers.

Billy grabs my hand, rubbing my arm. He is smug.

"Oh, really smooth skin. Does this myster-i-ous person like me?"

"I think the question is, Billy, do you like him or her?" Mrs. Dodgen replies.

"Do I?!" Billy answers, pulling off his blindfold. "More than any—"

He chokes, his eyes finding a little, black, hooty owl face before him.

But Billy didn't change. He chose to stand in the starkness and drink from its fear. Sometimes, a cripple doesn't show his cane, and sometimes, the only difference between a Christian and a heathen is how he says his prayers.

44

I see her in the hallway, walking slowly. The flat of her hand presses against the wall as she moves, steadying her body. She breathes as if winded, her pregnant belly bulging awkwardly in front of her. She stops to rest and I don't know if she can continue on. I see her again on the bloody birthing table, screaming. I close my eyes tightly, squeezing the image from my mind.

I hear the sharp snap of a trap springing, and a desperate, high-pitched squeal pierces the air. A silent sheet of dark crimson flows over the edge of the roof, cascading into a hollow darkness. A shimmering in the quiet of the falls fades to twisting red ribbons, and is lost.

He is struggling, trying to back away from this holy terror, but the strong coils press against his head without mercy. He fights, his hind feet kicking at the wooden base, the sounds of the struggle rattling through the wooden boards. My eyes are fixed on the scene, but flee briefly to the rafters for relief—or perhaps approval. I wonder if he is watching from above. Blood pours from the rat's nose and his eyes bulge out from his head. He glares at me through his struggle, hatred burning in his eyes even as he suffers.

I did nothing to you, they say. I never ventured to your side of the devil, you lousy hypocrite. I cared nothing for your loaves or fishes.

His legs twitch rapidly back and forth as he fights on his back, the trap cocked at an odd angle on top of him. His front paws scratch away at the trap as if he is drowning. The satchel at my side feels heavy and I see myself in my mind's light, cutting short his suffering by crushing his skull with a blow from the heavy crucifix. I gasp at this thought. I am sorry, Lord, for even thinking that could happen.

The heat kicks on, the vents expanding into the dull "boomp." It grows hot quickly near the metal ducts and the memories of a bouncing basketball become the hunting drums of a distant African village.

I am running through the grass of a savanna, my spear grasped tightly in one hand. My "Other" box is gone. I wear only a loincloth, and beads of sweat drip down my forehead as I sprint. My lungs surge forward, desperate to outrun my body, and drool hangs from my panting lips. I surprise my quarry and hurl my spear with every ounce of my strength. The metal point buries itself deep in his hairy side and he shrieks in pain. I grab the wooden shaft and hoist the spear up, my prize held high above my head. I feel it wiggling and look up. I am shocked to find the crucified man looking down at me, the point of my spear plunged deeply into the smooth skin of his side. His face betrays no pain, but his eyes question. I pull back the spear, horrified.

Noises behind me. The women have come to collect the meat. They swarm around him and jerk the cross from the ground. I try to stop them but I am waved away. The cross is laid out and lifted above the crowd, dozens of arms carrying the trophy to the village.

He is still now, the trap silent. In ancient times, animals were offered in homage, burned on altars of adoration. I pick up the tail and carry his lifeless body forward, setting him near the manger. At least he died knowing he was a rat. Some of us won't even get that pleasure. It is a grim reminder of the price for failure. I have offered up one of my own, but shiver beneath my robe, as if I am the one about to burn on the altar.

45

I try to watch the activity in the room below, but cannot.

The rat's violent death haunts me, but his passing has cleansed away an evil. And my triumph against this demon marks me as one who cleanses. I have become, like him, a healer.

A large hole appears in the roof between two of the rafters and bright sunlight floods the attic. I look out into an open sky, but something steals away the brightness. A makeshift litter is poked through the hole by ropes attached to poles, and a body rests on the litter. Unseen hands lower the litter further and the sunlight returns. I know who is coming—the paralytic man. I remember—he yearns to walk—to be freed from what binds him. His body descends further, the litter coming to rest on the floor of the catwalk. I gasp—it is the bed of the cross. And it is he, the nailed one, wanting to walk. To rise and go forth, seeking the dying.

I watch myself, the healer, walking into the light to kneel next to the cross. His crown is crooked, his head, tilted to one side to form an "f." I silently curse the inventor of that letter, and myself for its misuse, and I am grateful for closed eyes that do not fall upon my being. Every inch of his body contains gaping wounds and ugly bruises, and slivers of wood protrude like daggers from his back. Some of the bruises have turned dark, and I wonder if that is why purple is the color of kings. His body is covered in crimson, blood oozing from dozens of deep cuts in his skin. Red liquid flows in rivers from the nails in his hands, moving down his arms and dripping on the floor. The wound in his side oozes clear liquid.

The nails holding his hands and feet become pretty crimson marigolds, but return quickly to the truth. Not even my eyes can deny the scene I am witnessing, the bile welling from the pit of my being turning back the lie of doubt.

He has been lowered to me from above. No, he has lowered himself, and has come to the healer, seeking a freedom so he may heal.

But this has already been done, hasn't it? Two thousand years ago, he was freed from this cross, wasn't he? He was healed then, wasn't he? To go forth and heal? But then I remember, in this world of sand and water, the march of time is of no consequence.

I am the healer, and there is but one way for him to rise again. My hands grasp a silver pry bar with which I have bestowed false freedoms throughout my life. The thought of what I am about to do turns my stomach, but this deed must be done. The cup shall not pass. And this the only way I know how.

I slip the pry bar between his bloody hand and the wood of the cross until I feel resistance against the flesh. I turn my head from him and pull upward as I try not to retch. Even in death, he screams in pain, but his hand drops away, freed from the wood. I tell myself that this has already been done, that it is not really me performing the task. My actions merely reaffirm that this event did occur, his screams crying out across the ages. I move to the other side of his body and repeat my actions, freeing his other hand as he screams once more. I look down at the wounds in his palms. The gaping holes transcend the boundaries of time—that is the only way his act can be fulfilled. I am disgusted with myself as I look at his mangled hands. I did this, I alone, and there is no doubt on whom to lay the blame. Thomas, not even your eyes can miss it now.

I watch him as he lies there, his hands freed, blood pooled on the floor beneath the nails. He is motionless in the tragedy of the peace. And I, who chose to live in anger, am perhaps merely mad.

I hear screaming from below. His image gradually fades, leaving in its ghostly outline a final thought with me.

"You was well hated by those you loved, bro. Least I didn't cut your heart out."

Just broke it was all.

Desperate screams below me. Cries of the cross.

I see Mr. Devlin struggling, clutching his heart. He stumbles along the Other Wall, fighting his way toward the Not-So-Fun Room. I see him fall. Yelling in the hallway. He gets up and falls once more. Lots of yelling. I pull back, out of sight. Hundreds of goose bumps rise from an icy forest beneath my skin. I fear what's going on below. He falls for the third time. I know what's going on. More yelling, desperate and frantic.

The final drops of his blood fade from the catwalk floor. I rise from my knees, the healer summoned.

He stands at the door of his tomb, the early morning light creeping through cracks as the sun breaks the dawn. He waits between two seated lions, a hand resting on the head of each magnificent beast. His face tilts upward to his father.

"Dare I go forth?" he asks.

Silence stares down upon him.

"Dare I go forth?" he asks once more.

My foot reaches out into the black hole of my kingdom. I remove the satchel and lay the crucifix down. I will make this journey alone.

46

I push down on the backside of the Big White and the stairs spring open, the bottom step slamming hard against the hallway floor eight feet below. I have never looked down from Heaven before and the enormity of that burden weighs upon me now. I hesitate, but my foot drops through the opening and feels for the first step. My hand finds strength against a rafter, and as I steady myself, my other foot descends. My legs move down cautiously, a creaking sound betraying their presence as my one hundred and thirty pounds press against the wooden step. The skeleton of the rafters enclose me, and I'm feeling a bit like Jonah about to get vomited up. I grip my hand against the strength of the wood as the great fish rolls. I continue my descent, step by step, my eyes glued to the rafters until my tilted head emerges from the attic to the long hallway. I lower my gaze, freezing in mid-step.

The hallway is crowded with children who have come out of their classrooms. The entire student body is standing there, staring up at me, heads bobbing like dolls. I look into the faces of the children nearest to me. They show no fear, but much wonder, and their serenity puzzles me. I am a thief, a creature of dark skin who runs the black river, yet they are not afraid of me.

My eyes peer through the crowd, to the end of the hallway. It is not me they have come to see, I realize. Mr. Devlin lies on the floor near the Sacred Great Glass, a square of daylight shining upon him. He lies deathly still, open eyes staring up at the protruding box from which issues forth the Way and the Truth. Two teachers bend over his body.

"Mr. Devlin! Mr. Devlin!" I hear them shout frantically. "Can you hear us?"

The pregnant teacher has arrived and stands above them. She tries to bend down to her grandfather's body, but cannot. She straightens up, horrified, hands pressed against her face. Behind her, on the door to the Not-So-Fun Room, the red paper heart beats in the air of moving bodies.

I hear a shout.

"Somebody call an ambulance! For God's sake, somebody, please help!"

And all eyes turn to me, a million marbles rolling around innocently in heads too small to comprehend. Teachers and children are staring up at me. I descend the final step and stand among them. My feet move slowly forward, guided not by me, but by some power I do not understand. The children closest to me drop slowly to their knees, and farther up the hall, others follow their lead, until all along the length of the hallway, every child is kneeling. I move through them, passing the Children of the Knee who look up at me with hope in their eyes. They look up to see a small, flawed man robed in white with gold trim, who has emerged down the Stairway to Heaven. My hair radiates in the overhead lights—I can feel its warmth on my scalp. They are staring at the yellow light glowing around the head of this stranger, a man of dark skin, of scarring, blotchy freckles, of large brow and puffy lips, and frail of frame. I continue to walk up the hallway. It is surreal and I cannot feel my legs moving.

"It's God," a tiny, awed voice whispers as I pass by.

The message is passed, traveling up the hallway faster than I can walk. I hear it surging forward like an unstoppable wave.

"It's God."

"It's God."

It is not dirty yellow hair they see around my head. It is a halo.

"It's God."

"It's God."

"It's God."

The whispers cease, expressions of wonderment frozen on little faces. I look down to see a small, black face flashing a toothy smile. He beams up at me. A hooty owl who has just found out that God has black skin. A swelling of pride one cannot describe, but only relish.

The knot on my scalp tickles and I reach for it. My hand moves back down to my waist, palm open, a minute dot of blood clinging to a finger. Like father, like son. But they do not see it.

I walk past the doorways leading into the classrooms where I once sat, as they do now, and I am reminded of all the ideals I was taught as a student here. There I sit, my little head bent over a paper, my teeth gnawing on a pink eraser. But behind the pencils and basketballs, it was all about goodness. And I swept it all from me and quit, preferring to blame everyone else for my failures. Choosing instead to become a thief, lingering in a darkness greater than my own. And now I walk among them as God. A shame comes over me as I look down to see all I could have been and what I chose to be instead. All I twisted around to feed my hate. And I used my mama's only sin to justify the path I took and ignored everything else good she did in her life. What would she say to me now? I see her standing at the foot of a cross, dwarfed by a tall Roman centurion. The soldier offers up a wet sponge—and she an apple.

47

I stand above Mr. Devlin's body now, a million eyes on me.

"Save him, God," I hear a small voice beg. "Save him."

The two teachers rise from the floor and back away. They seem frightened of me but do not run. Tears flow from the eyes of the pregnant teacher. My mind is numb, but I kneel down next to the man's body. My hands press against his chest and I push, hard. I hear voices behind me.

"Our Father, who art in Heaven…"

They are praying. No one told them to. They just did.

"Hallowed be thy name…"

Reverence for he who watches over them. Respect. Hallowed, not hollow.

I stare down at his face. He has more wrinkles than when I knew him and his skin shows more wear. He is dead, and I know it. And there is no bringing him back.

"Thy kingdom come…"

It just did.

"Thy will be done…"

I push harder and faster on his chest. I am, after all, God.

His body jumps, I am pushing so hard. I stand on my knees and look down at him. His lips beckon me and I lean over and blow into his mouth. My breath is hot and it flows into him. His chest swells. I blow again. He lies still. My hands reach out and pull his body from the floor, sitting him up. I cradle his head between my hands and press my lips against his. As I do, my soul feels the kiss of a traitor long since gone, and I flinch. I close my eyes and blow, hard. I blow once more, my hands firmly against the sides of his head.

"Live," I command. "Live."

But I am an earthly God, limited in power. I cannot bring back the dead. Angered by my failure, I squeeze his head more forcefully between my hands. It's not supposed to be this difficult for one with the power.

"Help me," I ask.

I can feel my tears against his face.

"Live," I demand.

The body is limp in my care. I look down the hallway, to the rows of children. If he is dead, so then is God.

"Come back," I plead.

I pull back and look into the face between my hands. I gasp. I am holding mama's head. Her eyes are open and she stares blankly into the distance.

"Mama," I say.

She ignores me, searching into the infinity for something I cannot give. I have seen this look before.

"Mama!" I scream silently. "Don't be doing this to me again!"

I look into her lost face and it is too much for me to bear. I grab her and hold her against my body, cupping her head next to my own. She is limp, so very limp, but warm. I see her again, looking up at the cross. Her head turns and she looks over to a second cross. It is me hanging there on his left, my naked black skin exposed for the world to see. I am the thief punished with him.

She turns to me.

"Tell him," she demands, her face stern. "Make it right, boy."

I look over at him.

"What did I do?" I ask.

"Make it right, boy," she repeats. "You know what you did."

I look past him to see the donkey hanging from the cross to his right. He sneers at me, unrepentant, and I hate him for it. I look to the crucified man and then to mama.

"But he didn't do anything."

"That's right," she replies. "He did nothing. But you couldn't even do that much. And I'm dying from the shame."

I hug her body tighter against me, absorbing her, my eyes squeezing out the bitterness of the world I alone have created.

"For thine is the kingdom and the power and the glory..."

"I don't want to lose you twice, mama," I say. I lean toward her, my lips pressed against her ear and slowly whisper, "I am sorry."

I pull away to look into her face again. To make sure she understands. To tell her a second time. But she is gone. I stare into the

face of Mr. Devlin. His eyes are open, looking at me. A weak sound escapes from his mouth.
"Bitsy?"
A siren wails in the distance.

SIX MONTHS LATER

The world looks a little different through iron bars than it does through air vents. Although, I've got to tell you, looking at the world with your eyes straight ahead is a lot easier on the neck than bending your head, looking down all day. Yeah, that's right, they got me. It seems like the ambulance wasn't the only flashing light that showed up in front of the Sacred Great Glass that day.

I was ready to be cuffed—I just hadn't realized it. Sort of like getting my own cross lifted off my back and standing a little taller because of it. They did put the kids back in their classrooms before they put the silver bracelets on me, though—and for that, I am grateful. If one has to cuff God, it really should be a private affair.

The High Priests of Black and White were pretty nice to me, I will admit. They told me that, with my pretty white and gold robe, I was one of the best-dressed celebrities they'd ever had the honor to lock up. I fessed up to what I'd done, and with that over, I told it all—everything I'd ever done—every bit of it. It seemed to all just spill out. Funny, it seems the more I told 'em about all my pilfering over the years, the better I felt about coming clean—sort of like taking a bath that's been a long time coming. Mama would be proud—I know for a fact she would.

Boy, I bet the talk in the school carpool line that particular afternoon must have been something worth hanging around to hear. It seems that pregnant teacher, seeing her grandfather stretched out on the floor, and then God popping through the ceiling to save him, threw that poor mama-to-be right into labor. As they were cuffing me, they were shoving her into the back of the ambulance and shooing her off to the hospital. Grandpa had to wait 'til a second ambulance got there to get his ride. And with my little hang up about birthing, I was as nervous as an expectant father, watching that ambulance drive away with her in it. Her delivery was easy, she said, and Mom, Dad, and baby have visited me here in the joint—kind of nice of them, considering, don't you think? Mr. Devlin's been down here, too. He tells me he's just doing fine, calming words for both of us. I can't believe he remembered me after all those years. Must have been the hair, ya think? He even fixed it so I get to keep my pretty God robe, and it'll be waiting for me when I get out. It will be quite a souvenir. I'm gonna enjoy Mr. Devlin while I got him, and be grateful, 'cause if it hadn't been for all of this, our separate lives would have just passed on by just like they were headed, and I would still be running the black river. For now, I'll accept my peace a little at a time and just hope the rest of the puzzle will come together in due time.

    The judge listened to my story, 'bout the donkey running off while the horse stayed, and my old principal, Mrs. Babcock, hobbled into the courtroom with a shiny oak walking stick to tell him what I said was the God's truth. I even told them how I'd done my first job—that I'd just picked up a Baby Ruth candy bar that had fallen on the floor of the Westside Grocery, and how that hadn't seemed to hurt anyone—it had been stepped on anyhow—and how that heist had worked out so well that I just started pinching stuff from higher up on the shelf. They all got a laugh when the judge told me that at least working that way, I didn't have to worry about throwing my back out, you know, by bending way over for the lower pickings.

    Come to find out, I had been a martyr only to myself, and that's an awful lot of work to please an audience that small. Ever try nailing one hand to a cross with the other? It doesn't work very well. When I think about it, though, it kind of warms my heart that Jesus felt more at home hanging next to a thief when he could have picked a lawyer. I do find some justice in knowing that. Now, when I get up in the morning, I look at myself in the mirror and smile—two things I didn't used to do much. I even got my own private joke I use in the prison lunch line. Once in a while, when someone asks me if I'd like coffee, I just grin and tell them no—I'm getting the "t." Nobody else thinks that's particularly funny, though.

    I had been so terrified all my days by the unjust pain of bringing new life into this world that I had never stopped to think about the great rewards involved in actually doing so. Sometimes, confusion is in the answer and not in the question, and I'll abide by that explanation for right now. But I don't think I'm that way anymore. For I witnessed a birth right there in that hallway of the Second Street Christian

School. It is truly an amazing thing, a new life. For what needs to walk forth, does. And a spirit that should be, is. And even in its silence, it teaches.

www.ingramcontent.com/pod-product-compliance
Lightning Source LLC
Chambersburg PA
CBHW022305060426
42446CB00007BA/592